NEW HALL

David Holgate

faber and faber

LONDON · BOSTON

First published in 1971 as *New Hall and Its Imitators*
by Faber and Faber Limited
3 Queen Square London WC1N 3AU

This completely revised, rewritten and expanded edition first published in 1987

Filmset by Wilmaset Birkenhead Wirral
Printed in Great Britain by
Jolly & Barber Ltd Rugby Warwickshire
All rights reserved

British Library Cataloguing in Publication Data

Holgate, David
New Hall. —— 2nd rev. ed.
1. New Hall porcelain —— Collectors and collecting
I. Title
738.2′7   NK4399.N4
ISBN 0−571−18072−8

for

KIT

NEW HALL

THE FABER MONOGRAPHS ON POTTERY AND PORCELAIN

Present Editors: R. J. Charleston and Margaret Medley

Former Editors: W. B. Honey, Arthur Lane
and Sir Harry Garner

FOREWORD

The first edition of this book appeared in 1971. Since that date a considerable amount of new evidence bearing on the history of the New Hall factory has come to light, and many new wares have been discovered which may be attributed to the factory and which expand our notions of its production. David Holgate has himself often been the discoverer, as he was the first person to give us a rounded picture of what New Hall porcelain really was. Now that this is established, he has been able to discard from the present book the detailed discussion which in the first edition was devoted to the other factories which made wares in New Hall style. This has allowed him to concentrate on New Hall itself and greatly to expand his earlier text. His list of numbered patterns has also been much extended. Readers of the earlier work will certainly feel impelled to read its successor.

R. J. CHARLESTON

FOREWORD TO 1971 EDITION

Porcelain-manufacture in England has followed a different course from that in other countries. Whereas in Germany and Italy, and subsequently in France too, porcelain in the eighteenth century was made in a modified version of the 'true' or 'hard-paste' ware of the Orient, composed of china-clay and china-stone, in England various forms of 'soft-paste' porcelain were made. These in general gave way ultimately to a formula in which bone-ash played an important part as a constituent, this body finally evolving into the 'bone-china' which since the end of the eighteenth century has been, and still is, the distinctive English porcelain. The exception to this general development has been the isolated episode of the production of hard-paste porcelain, first at Plymouth, then at Bristol and finally at New Hall in Staffordshire. All these factories were related and succeeded one another. The New Hall concern itself was finally forced to give up hard-paste porcelain and to turn to the more economic bone-china body. Its recognition of commercial realities also affected form and decoration. Whereas the Bristol factory had aspired to styles as elaborate as those of any of its contemporaries, the New Hall factory, after an ambitious start, realised that its true market lay in the middle ranges of society. It therefore concentrated on simpler and cheaper styles of decoration for a wider clientele. In consequence, considerable quantities of New Hall porcelain have survived, and their relative simplicity has until fairly recently preserved them from the attentions of the collector and connoisseur. Now, when the search for early English porcelain of all sorts has become fiercely competitive, the balance has been redressed, and New Hall is eagerly collected. A comprehensive and discriminating book on the subject is therefore overdue.

Mr Holgate has devoted many years of study and collecting activity to his chosen subject, but has not allowed his concentration to make him narrow-minded. A most useful feature of this book is that he does not exclude from his survey the wares of other factories often mistaken for those of New Hall. It should therefore prove particularly welcome to collectors who have turned to this field on account of the relative cheapness and availability of the porcelains of this type. He has rendered a great service in clarifying a hitherto confused chapter in the history of porcelain-making in England.

R. J. CHARLESTON

COLOUR PLATES

CONTENTS

PREFACE

It was a privilege to have *New Hall and Its Imitators* published in 1971 by Faber and Faber in their series of monographs on ceramics. At that time New Hall was the Cinderella of the early English porcelain factories and many collectors turned away when the name was mentioned. In fact it was more a generic term for a class of porcelain than descriptive of the products of a single factory. I attempted to separate the sheep from the goats and to indicate guide lines for identifying New Hall wares and distinguishing them from the many similar pots which were the products of other factories. I never thought my missionary work would be quite so successful and I have frequently been humbled at the sight of copies so well used as to be almost falling apart. In fact New Hall porcelain is so keenly collected, and so much has been written about the other contemporary porcelain makers, that it has seemed more suitable, now that the original book is out of print, to rewrite it as a tribute to New Hall alone. The wares can be described in more detail and the range of the pattern book extended. The increased number of illustrations and the opportunity to include pictures within the text has enabled me to describe the development of the shapes of the wares with the text and pictures together: similarly with the pattern book. However, in order to illustrate a wider range, I have not always repeated a pattern once it has been shown elsewhere. Some compromise has been necessary. There are two principal reasons for there being more space devoted to the hard-paste wares than to the bone-china. Undoubtedly the greatest enthusiasm is found amongst the collectors of hard-paste: there is a wider range of attractive pots for them and besides, these are the earlier products from the years of challenge. Secondly, as I have indicated in the text, we are only just beginning to realise the full extent of the bone-china production; as a scientist, I am pleased to say there is scope for research here and further careful study is needed.

ACKNOWLEDGEMENTS

Knowledge and understanding of a subject cannot be gained unaided and the accumulation of material for a book requires the help, co-operation and goodwill of many people. I have been particularly fortunate in this respect, and I appear to have lost no friends despite, after frequent visits, leaving their collections in Babylonian confusion. Some of my debts can never be repaid adequately. Geoffrey Godden has been particularly kind and generous, always giving me the freedom of his remarkable collections. I value his friendship. Mrs Geoffrey Grey kindly gave me access to her husband's records after his sad death. Amongst the many individuals who have contributed to my knowledge I must express my thanks to Pat and Michael Auburn, Peter Davis, Roger Edmondson, Mr and Mrs A. de Saye Hutton, Eileen and Rodney Hampson, Nick Lazarus, Dr and Mrs V. E. Lloyd Hart, Joyce McCarthy, Field McIntyre, Philip Miller, Mrs Barbara Peterson, Roger Pomfret, Valerie Thomas and Mr and Mrs W. L. Woodage. It is possible that some of the illustrated pieces are in collections which are unknown to me and therefore their owner has not been acknowledged; I apologise if this should have happened. It has been impossible to trace the whereabouts of some of the pots which were in my collection when it was sold at Sotheby's. I hope the many antique dealers who have helped me will take pleasure when they see some of the pieces they sold. Museum staff have always been keen to help and I am grateful to the curators, keepers and staff at the Usher Gallery, Lincoln, Luton Art Gallery and Museum, Norwich Castle Museum and the Victoria and Albert Museum as well as Mr F. B. Stitt, the Staffordshire county archivist at the William Salt Library, Stafford. I particularly want to mention Arnold Mountford, the director of the City Museum and Art Gallery, Stoke-on-Trent; for more than twenty years I have had every encouragement and assistance from him, a high point for me being the honour of being invited to mount the New Hall Bicentenary Exhibition in 1981 in his galleries. The staff of many auctioneers, especially of Christie's, Phillips and Sotheby's, have informed me of important items in their sales and provided me with photographs; in this context I particularly want to thank Paul Mack of Sotheby's at Chester for his generous help. I am indebted to Dr Ian Fraser of Keele University for being so helpful when I consulted the relevant bills and letters in the Wedgwood Archives. It is generous of Messrs Wedgwood of Barlaston and Messrs Hand, Morgan and Owen of Stafford, the owners of the New Hall documents, to make them available for study. I must also thank Robert Charleston, the editor of the Faber Monographs, for his advice and guidance when this book was in its formative stages, and Giles de la Mare, who has been very patient with me over the many delays.

Finally, I want to thank my son Robin and my wife Kit for their constant encouragement: without Kit's shared interest and enthusiasm for ceramics and the eighteenth century this book could not have been written.

CHAPTER I

Introduction

For fifty years, between 1781 and 1835, the New Hall China Works made porcelain tea-sets for the Englishman's table. We cannot seriously study their place in ceramic history or gain a true perspective until we have considered how tea-drinking and tea-wares became a part of the English way of life.

Until the eighteenth century ale was brewed in this country and drunk almost universally by the working man; more refined families were raised on port, claret and other wines. Although tea was first imported into Europe (Holland) early in the seventeenth century (1610), its use was mainly medicinal, and its social possibilities were not appreciated until the end of the century; for instance, in 1657 tea as a drink was first sold in London coffee-houses as a cure for 'Giddiness, weakness of the Stomach, Agues and Feavers' and leaf-tea was sold by chemists and not by grocers. It was Catherine of Braganza's arrival, at the end of the Commonwealth with the Restoration of Charles II, that made it an acceptable and popular drink at court and amongst the aristocracy. Now the scene was set for the expansion of tea-drinking, which neither increasing levies and taxes nor social attitudes could prevent.[1]

Once the taste for tea and the habit of drinking it had spread, the need for tea-wares was created. The first porcelain tea-wares were made in China and imported

[1] In 1695 a tax of a shilling in the pound was imposed on lawfully imported tea and 1s 6d in the pound on unlawfully imported tea, i.e. that which did not arrive in ships of the East India Company. This was doubled in 1704 and increased again in 1712.

Dr Johnson admitted 'that tea is a liquor not proper for the lower classes of the people, as it supplies no strength to labour, or relief to disease, but gratifies the taste without nourishing the body'; Dorothy Bradshaigh built and endowed a rural almshouse in 1775 and strictly forbade tea to its occupants.

by the East India Company with the tea leaves. The need to import them generated the stimulus and presented the challenge: why pay more to import what you can make yourself?

Successful commercial manufacture of porcelain depends upon a number of factors: the availability of suitable raw materials and a knowledge of the technology to use them, a willing market, and transport to carry the raw materials to the factory and the finished ware to the customer. In the 1740s, when the first pieces of English porcelain were made, at Bow and Chelsea in London and at Newcastle-under-Lyme in Staffordshire, London was the centre for tea-drinking. It must have been the closeness to their customers and the ease of importing raw materials that made Bow and Chelsea more successful.

It does seem curious that in spite of their supreme ability to make pottery Staffordshire potters were unable to make porcelain a successful enterprise before 1780. Even Longton Hall (1751–60), which made porcelain tea-wares and figures of high quality, could not market its wares successfully. The most likely explanation must lie in the ease or difficulty of transport; Lowestoft, Bristol and Liverpool had immediate access to the sea, Worcester and Caughley were on the navigable River Severn, and Derby was connected by canal to the River Trent. Only Stoke-on-Trent was handicapped by ineffectual road transport; sixteen miles to the canal at Winsford in Cheshire and thirty miles to Willington near Derby.[2]

As the eighteenth century drew to an end the Industrial Revolution was well under way and a dramatic social change was taking place – a change which was to have a marked effect upon tea-drinking in England and porcelain manufacture in Staffordshire. The new industrial society not only increased the number of tea-drinkers but set their homes in the industrial centres of the north, far from the social hub of London. Furthermore, the Trent and Mersey Canal was opened in 1777, so

---

[2]A petition supporting 'high-road' improvements was presented to the House of Commons on 16 February 1763: 'This petition, of the several towns and villages, and of several merchants and traders residing in Newcastle-under-Lyme . . . sets forth, that the road from the Red Bull to Lawton, Cheshire to and thro Killigrew (Kidsgrove) Goldenhill, Tunstall, Burslem, Cobridge, Hanley and Shelton to Cliff Bank near Stoke-upon-Trent, is in a ruinous condition and in many places ponderous, narrow and incommodious, and at each end falls into a great Turnpike road, leading to Winsford ferries, and at the other end into a Turnpike leading to Uttoxeter, and so on to Willington Ferry, where the navigation to Gainsborough and Hull commences, whereby the materials for the manufacture of earthenware are chiefly brought and conveyed, and the manufactured goods are chiefly carried to markets, whereby great profits and advantage arise, in case the said communication between the said Turnpikes was made easy and passable for carriages. That some of the petitioners have already subscribed the sum of £1,200 for and towards the repairs, and only wait for the power of erecting Turnpikes to reimburse them and to complete the said roads.'

that Staffordshire potters could now compete on equal terms with any other potter in the country. The dice that had seemed loaded against Longton Hall now rolled to the advantage of the potters who combined to form the china manufactory which was later to be called New Hall.

CHAPTER 2

The Patent Comes to Staffordshire

Continental potters, with wealthy and sometimes royal patronage, found ways of making porcelain in the late sixteenth and seventeenth centuries. Inspired by this success, aspiring porcelain makers in England sought suitable raw materials. The general principles of the manufacture were widely, if not generally, known with the publication in Paris, in 1735, of 'Description . . . de l'empire de la Chine' by B. J. B. Du Halde, a Jesuit missionary. This contained a description of the composition and manufacture of Chinese porcelain. Certainly the potters in Staffordshire were aware of it. John Wedgwood, traditionally known as the 'earth potter', of the Big House, Burslem, wrote about the technique of Chinese porcelain manufacture in August 1743, in 'An Essay on Pottery'.[1]

Combining documentary evidence and archaeological excavation, Mr Paul Bemrose, the curator of Newcastle-under-Lyme Museum, and Mr Arnold Mountford, director of the City of Stoke-on-Trent Museums, have shown that porcelain was being made in Staffordshire in about 1745 by at least two groups of potters.[2] In 1970, Mr Bemrose's team digging on the Pomona Potworks site in Lower Street, Newcastle-under-Lyme, unearthed kilns and a large quantity of 'sherds amongst which was a bowl dated on the base "26 July 1746"'. These Staffordshire potters may not have been commercially successful but they were, nevertheless, making porcelain at the same time as the better-known London potters at Chelsea and Bow. However, none of these early porcelain makers used the same

[1]A. R. Mountford, *E.C.C. Trans.*, vol. 7, part 2, 1969, pp. 96–9.

[2]A. R. Mountford, op. cit., pp. 87–95. Paul Bemrose, *E.C.C. Trans.*, vol. 9, part 1, 1973, pp. 1–18.

raw materials as the Chinese. Despite the knowledge that in China the translucency was achieved by the use of a form of a stone (called at various times 'petuntse', 'growan-stone', 'moor-stone' and 'china-stone') all the early English factories used a different material, chiefly glass. Thus these early porcelains have been classed as 'artificial', to distinguish them from the 'real' or 'true' porcelain made by the Chinese.

In 1737, an American potter, Andrew Duché,[3] who was living in Savannah, Georgia, claimed to have found both the materials and the method to make porcelain. He sought financial aid from the Trustees for the Settlement of Carolina and Georgia. Despite his ability to interest some of the local officials, support was insufficient and in May 1743 he came to England; whether it was to sell the secrets of manufacture or his sources of raw materials, we cannot be certain. There is no positive record of the company that Duché kept once he set foot in England. On the other hand, it seems probable that he met Edward Heylyn and Thomas Frye in London, since they took out their patents in 1744 and 1745 mentioning 'an earth, the product of the Cherokee nation in America called by the Natives unaker'. On the other hand, as the son of a Huguenot potter, he is a very strong candidate for identification as the visitor to William Cookworthy in Plymouth recorded in the following letter, dated 30 May 1745, to Cookworthy's friend Richard Hingston, surgeon at Penryn:[4]

> I had, lately with me, the person who hath discovered the China-earth. He had several samples of the China-ware, of their making, with him; which were, I think, equal to the Asiatic. 'Twas found in the back of Virginia where he was in quest of mines; and having read Du Halde, discovered both the Petunse and Kaulin. 'Tis this latter earth, he says, is the essential thing towards the success of the Manufacture. He is gone for a Cargo of it, having bought the whole country of the Indians, where it rises. They can import it for £13 per Ton, and by that means, afford their China as cheap as common stone ware. But they intend only to go about 30 per cent. under the Company. The man is a Quaker by profession, but seems to be as thorough a Deist, as I ever met with. He knows a good deal of mineral affairs, but not *funditus*.

William Cookworthy was a distinguished Quaker minister and a chemist who, after qualifying in London, returned to his native Plymouth and, being fluent in

[3]Graham Hood, 'The Career of Andrew Duché', *Art Quarterly*, XXXI, No. 2, 1968, pp. 168–84.

[4]F. Severne Mackenna, *E.C.C. Trans.*, vol. 11, part 2, 1982, p. 89.

several languages, was a natural focus for visitors to this port. At some time, perhaps after meeting Duché, he became interested in making porcelain and finding the necessary materials with which to make it. It is unfortunate that the following memorandum[5] is undated but, given that he died in 1780, it must surely have been between 1750 and 1760:

> It is now near Twenty years since I discover'd that the Ingredients used by the Chinese in the Composition of their porcelain, were to be got, in immense quantities, in the County of Cornwall; . . . I first discovered the petuntse in the Parish of Germo, in a hill called Tregonin Hill . . . There are inexhaustible stores of Caulin in the two Western Counties. . . . The sort [caulin], I have chiefly tried, is what is got from the side of Tregonin Hill, where there are several pits of it. . . . I have lately discovered that, in the neighbourhood of the parish of St Stephen's in Cornwall, there are immense quantities both of the Petunse stone and the Caulin, and which, I believe, may be more commodiously and advantageously wrought than those of Tregonin Hill . . .

His first attempt at making porcelain was at Bristol between 7 November and 15 December 1765, but his main efforts were made in Plymouth. Thomas Pitt, on whose land Cookworthy found large quantities of china-clay and china-stone, gave his encouragement as well as financial support.[6]

On 17 March 1768, Cookworthy was granted a patent for the manufacture of porcelain and in this year two companies were formed to exploit it: the Plymouth New Invented Porcelain Company (at Coxside, Plymouth) and William Cookworthy and Company (at Castle Green, Bristol) in partnership with Richard Champion amongst others. The manufacturing process seems always to have been beset with problems and while Cookworthy by continual experiment diagnosed the problems, their successful solution eluded him. Rarely, if ever, was a whole kiln of porcelain perfect.

In 1770 the Plymouth works were closed and all efforts were concentrated in the Bristol Company. It is possible that Thomas Pitt wished to withdraw his support, for in this year he granted Cookworthy a ninety-nine years' lease on his land for the

[5]George Harrison, *Memoir of William Cookworthy*, 1854, Appendix V. Ll. Jewitt, *The Ceramic Art of Great Britain*, 1878, vol. 1, pp. 323–6.

[6]Letters from Cookworthy to Thomas Pitt are deposited in the Cornwall County Record Office, Truro (reference: DFF(4)80, 1–27). They are published in *Apollo*, December 1980 and January 1981: 'The Plymouth Porcelain Factory, Letters to Thomas Pitt, 1766–69'.

supply of the raw materials. There was a covenant '. . . that he, the said Thomas Pitt and his heirs should not during the time permit any Moor Stone or Gravel, being on any estate or land belonging to him to be raised and used for the making of porcelain and china other than by virtue of this lease upon penalty of £20 for every ton'. This covenant and the lease were to cause Richard Champion, the Bristol merchant, considerable trouble in later years.

In 1774 Cookworthy himself withdrew from the scene, and the Bristol works, together with the patent, were sold to Richard Champion on 6 May. In 1790, Thomas Pitt, who by this time was Lord Camelford, wrote to a Mr Polwhele thus about the Plymouth venture:[7]

> With regard to the Porcelain Manufactory, that was attempted to be established some years ago and which was afterwards transferred to Bristol, where it failed; it was undertaken by a Mr Cookworthy upon a friend of his having discovered on an estate of mine in the Parish of St Stephen's, a certain white saponaceous clay; and close by it a species of granite or moorstone, white with greenish spots; which he immediately perceived to be the two materials described by the Missionary Père d'Entrecolles, as the constituent parts of the Chinese porcelain; the one giving whiteness and body to the paste, the other vitrefication and transparency. The difficulties found in proportioning properly these materials, so as to give exactly the necessary degree of vitrefication, and no more, and other niceties with regard to the manipulation, discouraged us from proceeding in this concern; after we had procured a patent for the use of our materials and expended on it between two and three thousand pounds. We then sold our interest to Mr Champion of Bristol.

Like Cookworthy, Richard Champion, to whom this patent and the Castle Green works were sold in 1774, was a Quaker. Unlike Cookworthy, however, he was neither a chemist nor a ceramist. His lack of suitable experience was decried by Wedgwood some years later. It is obvious that Champion did not buy an established manufacturing process, for within a year, in 1775, he was applying to Parliament for an extension of fourteen years to the life of the patent. He also hoped to obtain a monetary grant. The extension was bitterly opposed by Wedgwood on behalf of the Staffordshire potters, not just because it prevented other potters from making true porcelain but because it restricted the use of the raw materials in any ceramic product. Rarely can there have been such a tactical struggle for such a seemingly

[7]H. Owen, *Two Centuries of Ceramic Art in Bristol*, 1873, p. 77.

innocent bill. Champion gave presents of his porcelain, and Wedgwood was rebuked by the House for distributing, within the Commons, a 'Memorial relative to the Petition from Mr Champion for the extension of a Patent on behalf of himself, and the manufacturers of earthenware in the County of Stafford against the said Bill'. Unashamedly Wedgwood burst into print thrice more when the bill proceeded to the Lords: 'Remarks upon Mr Champion's reply to Mr Wedgwood's "Memorial on behalf of himself and the Potters in Staffordshire" ', a sheet of 'Reasons why the extension of the term of Mr Cookworthy's Patent by authority of Parliament would be injurious to many landowners, to the manufacturers and the public', and 'The case of the manufacturers of earthenware in Staffordshire'.

The outcome was a compromise. At the Parliament 'begun and holden at *Westminster*, the Twenty-ninth day of *November, Anno Domini* 1774' Champion gained his extension which was 'from and after the End and Expiration of the said Term of Fourteen Years thereby granted, for and during the further or additional Term of Fourteen Years' (i.e. an extension from 1782 until 1796), but he conceded two amendments. He agreed to supply 'a specification of the mixture and proportions of the raw materials of which his porcelain is composed and likewise . . . the glaze of the same,' within four months, and he conceded that any potter could use the materials except 'in such proportions as are in the specification herein directed'. While Champion was able to enrol an acceptable specification which disclosed no secrets, the concession on the use of the raw materials was important because it allowed the potters to import the materials and acquire skill and practice in handling them. It also led to the discovery of alternative sources of supply, which resulted, as always, in price competition.

The cost of extending the patent was high and probably dashed any hopes which Champion had of making his manufacture of porcelain profitable. Production at Bristol was at a low ebb in 1778 and Champion began to seek a way out. Wedgwood, writing to Bentley on 24 August 1778, observed that 'poor Champion is quite demolished . . . he had neither professional knowledge, sufficient capital, nor any real acquaintance with the materials he was working with'. Wedgwood contemptuously talked about buying raw materials from him at a low price but Champion never suffered this humiliation. Wedgwood must have been greatly surprised when in 1780 Champion approached him with a proposition for making china in Staffordshire. On 12 November 1780, Wedgwood wrote to his partner Bentley:[8]

[8]This letter and other Wedgwood documents are kept in Keele University Library and are reproduced by kind permission of Messrs Wedgwood of Barlaston.

Amongst other things Mr Champion of Bristol has taken me up near two days. He is come amongst us to dispose of his secret – His patent etc. and, who could have believed it? has chosen me for his friend and confidante. I shall not deceive him for I really feel much for his situation. A wife and eight children (to say nothing of himself) to provide for, and out of what I fear will not be thought of much value here – The secret of China making. He tells me he has sunk fifteen thousand pounds in this gulf, and his idea is now to sell the whole art, mystery, and patent for six, and he is now trying a list of names I have given him of the most substantial and enterprising potters amongst us, and will acquaint me with the event.

I gave him reasons why I could not be concerned in such a partnership which I believe were satisfactory even to himself.

The points at the end of Wedgwood's letter deserve further study. On what basis were the potters selected, and why was Wedgwood not prepared to participate in any scheme? Was he disinterested or disenchanted? In 1773, before its assignment to Champion, an obviously curious Wedgwood had asked Bentley (3 April 1773) to let him have a copy of Cookworthy's patent, saying: 'It may be of consequence to know everything about this Patent before we begin to make white tea ware.' Immediately after the parliamentary battles Wedgwood accompanied by John Turner went to Cornwall in search of clay and stone, intent upon obtaining these raw materials for research purposes. In a series of letters to Bentley, Wedgwood explained that Turner and he had obtained materials, and that after washing them they would make them generally available. In fact there was a general meeting of potters at 'Moretons on the Hill' when a research association was proposed and an agreement drawn up 'to improve our present manufacture and make a useful white porcelain body with a colourless glaze for the same'.

A postscript to a letter written by Wedgwood to Sir John Wrottesley on 29 November 1775 says:

I am much oblig'd to you for your kind inquiries after our success with the Growan Stone and Clay, and should have inclos'd you a copy of Mr Champion's very curious Specification, but it is not made out, so must defer it to another post.

We have made some progress in our improvements with the Cornish Materials, but not much, as we wait for the establishment of a Public Experimental work, which I hope will take place soon. We had a meeting of the Potters yesterday upon the subject, when I deliver'd in a Plan which was approv'd of, and it was agreed to put it into execution so soon as proper Buildings and other conveniences could be prepared for the purpose.

A few days later he had bad news for Bentley:

To Mr Bentley

Dec. 1775

I minute down a few memorandums to my Dear Friend *as laconic* as possible to encroach as little upon his precious time as may be.

Your Socratic Familiar has not deceiv'd you – Our Experimental work expir'd in Embryo last night. We could not settle the question whether the Partners in Company should pay separately, or jointly as Mr Byerly wrote you before. I consented to agree to either plan, being determin'd it should not fail on my account, for I thought myself bound in honour to the Gentlemen who Patronised our opposition to Champion's Bill to give the plan a fair trial. My inclination too accompanied my engagement to the Gentlemen, as I heartily wish a general improvement to the Manufacture. But it seems it cannot be in this way, and having done my duty I am contented, and shall take my own course quietly by myself as well as I can, and may perhaps have it in my power to serve the trade some other way.

I should not have troubled you with this account, but as you may be asked concerning this plan or its failure, I wish you to be able to give them an answer.

I shall now begin with the materials in earnest, I scarcely thought my self at liberty to do so whilst the Partnership plan was in agitation – Pray consult your Familiar for me, and let me hear, that I may obey the Oracle. . . .

Yours most affectionately
Jos. Wedgwood

This inability to forge agreement amongst his fellow potters was no doubt partly responsible for Wedgwood's not taking up Champion's offer when it came, but it certainly did not prevent him from carrying out his own research. This research gave him a deep insight into the methods and problems of making porcelain. Almost insuperable to his mind was the inconsistent quality and composition of the moor- (or china-) stone so that 'I despair of making it a Principle ingredient in a Porcelain Manufactory, and unless the Bristol People alter their principle I do not think it possible for them to succeed'.[9] Any lingering thoughts that may have been in his mind of making porcelain at this time were dispelled a fortnight later. On 6 February he told Bentley 'I do not wish to purchase any English process, and much less the bone, which I think one of the worst processes for china making.'

In April 1781, following Wedgwood's rejection of his advances, Champion published an Address which he circulated among the Staffordshire potters.[10] It gave his reasons for wishing to move to Staffordshire from Bristol and suggested 'forming an extensive work in Shares by Subscription, open to the Country'. There must have been an immediate response and some of the questions raised by the interested potters were the subject of correspondence between Champion and Cookworthy's descendants.[11] The principle stumbling block was that Champion was not free to make a simple proposition to the potters since he was legally bound to buy raw materials from Lord Camelford, which would probably be more expensive than could be bought elsewhere and he had to pay a further premium on them to Cookworthy's descendants. These problems were raised and his future intentions outlined in letters. Finally in the one to Mr George Harrison[12] Champion said, 'I have now entered into an agreement with ten Potters only.' Unfortunately it is not clear what Champion's part was to be. One interpretation is that, funded by the potters, he would show them how to make porcelain and then allow them, and any others, to use the method in their own works. In effect Champion would not be making porcelain and would then be freed from any restrictions on the source of the raw materials. On the other hand, this freedom could be obtained also if he sold the patent outright to a new company and was installed as the manager. Since he left Staffordshire precipitately, and John Daniel was made the manager of the venture from an early date, it is more likely that the latter course was taken.

Further details of Champion's negotiations in Staffordshire are found in letters written by his sister Sarah. In one dated 4 June 1781[13] she says, 'my brother, who with my sister, the 4th of this month returned from London in their road from Staffordshire, are with all the family at Henbury, which place he proposes to dispose of very soon, intending for some time to come to make Newcastle in Staffordshire

[9]Appendix I, 1, p. 222–3, for the full text of this letter.

[10]Appendix I, 2, pp. 223–6, for the full text of the Address.

[11]Appendix I, 3 (a)–(d), pp. 226–30, for the text of the letters which were published first by R. J. Charleston in *Connoisseur*, April 1956, p. 186.

[12]Appendix I, 3 (c), p. 228–9.

[13]H. Owen, op. cit., p. 199.

the place of their residence, he being in a way of profitably disposing of the China manufactory reserving a part to himself.' Champion travelled to Staffordshire on 5 November 1781[14] and lived in Merrill Street (now Merrial Street) in Newcastle-under-Lyme until 6 April. Then he accepted a political post which took him initially to London and finally to America, where he died. Whilst it may not seem surprising to us that this man, who was originally a merchant in Bristol, should be willing to turn to the new life offered to him, it was not his original idea. There seems little doubt that he intended to be in Staffordshire for some time, since on 18 March, less than a month before leaving, he took out an insurance policy on the contents of his house and on a laboratory.[15] He would hardly have a laboratory nor 'Utensils and Stock in Trade consisting of Cobbalt and Blue Colour prepared therein' if he had not been in earnest.

[14]H. Owen, op. cit., p. 199.

[15]Appendix I, 4, p. 230–1.

CHAPTER 3

The Members of the New Hall Company

Wedgwood gave Champion a list of names of 'the most substantial and enterprising potters amongst us' and Champion said that he came to agreement with 'ten potters only'. In 1810, when the copyhold was bought, these ten were reduced to four: Samuel Hollins, Peter Warburton, John Daniel, and William Clowes (and two of these were not original partners). After his attempt to start a research association had foundered, Wedgwood would know who was really interested in making porcelain and which of these had a co-operative mind. Doubtless the list of names given to Champion contained many, if not all, of those involved with his earlier attempt to investigate the art of porcelain making. There would be a number of refusals before the number became ten, and today, because we have none of the original documents available, these ten names are not known with certainty. The earliest known document mentioning names is a leasehold agreement dated 1 March 1803 and it lists eight (John Hollins, gentleman; Samuel Hollins, potter; Peter Warburton, potter; William Clowes, gentleman; Joshua Heath and Charles Bagnall, gentlemen; and John Daniel, potter); whilst early ceramic writers (Shaw and Jewitt) say that when Champion left, 'a disagreement ensued amongst the partners: Mr Keeling and Mr John Turner withdrew and they who continued together engaged as managing partner Mr John Daniel'. Since Daniel was not an original name, we know therefore only a possible eight of the original ten men. Perhaps more than two left with Champion?

In later chapters I shall write about the life of the factory and its wares but it seems timely now to look at the men who started the enterprise and nurtured it until it became an established success.

JOHN TURNER
born 1738, died 1787

The son of a lawyer, John Turner was a first-generation potter. Even so he was one of the most skilful and enterprising potters in Staffordshire. His stoneware, caneware, basaltes and jasperware products stand alongside those of Wedgwood. He was successful. Why did he help to found New Hall and yet retire before the venture had really begun? Some of his activities and achievements in this connection are enigmas.

In 1775, with Josiah Wedgwood, he represented the Staffordshire potters in opposing the extension of Champion's hard-paste patent. Then in 1781 he was a member of the consortium of potters who negotiated with Champion and bought this same hard-paste patent – an apparent *volte-face*. However, it has been suggested that Turner was sent by the Staffordshire potters to keep an eye on Wedgwood's activities rather than to fight for their belief in their freedom to use the raw materials.[1] No doubt Turner, like many potters, yearned to make porcelain, and, being adventurous and capable, he took the opportunity when it arose.

A document which was amongst the New Hall property deeds when G. E. Stringer wrote his book in 1949 gives the following information (page 11):

Manor of Newcastle-under-Lyme
Surrender of 7th July, 1779

'To this Court comes John Hollins of Newcastle aforesaid, mercer, Ralph Baddely of Shelton, potter, and Thomas Smith of Penkhull, gent., all of the County of Stafford, and surrender into the hands of the Lord of the said Manor all that Messuage called Shelton Hall with the little croft thereto adjoining and all potworks, barns, stables, gardens, hereditaments and appurtenances to the same belonging, and also all those closes and pieces of land to the same adjoining, late the estate of Alice Dalton, and called the Hall Meadows, the Middle Field, the Aslams Patch, the Clover Field, Miles' Meadow, the Near Bryans Wood, the Middle Bryans Wood and the Further Bryans Wood, including the oatfield and all ways, watercourses and appurtenances to the same belonging, To the use and behoof of John Turner of Lane End in the County of Stafford, Potter, for the term of 99 years if Humphrey Palmer late of Hanley, potter, shall so long live.'

[1] Bevis Hillier, *The Turners of Lane End*, 1965, p. 34.

We do not know what was in Turner's mind when he leased this property but Mr Stringer suggested that it was done in preparation for making porcelain in partnership with Champion: for, if Shaw and Jewitt are right, we do know that Turner was one of the group of potters who combined to buy the Champion hard-paste patent and that both he and Keeling withdrew when Champion left to further his political career. We do not know why Turner and Keeling left but it is curious to find that when Turner left he allowed the remaining potters to use Shelton Hall for the manufacture of hard-paste porcelain.

Turner's career after this episode does not come into the story of New Hall but since there is a marked mug in the City of Stoke-on-Trent Museum and since the 'Gerverot beaker'[2] decorated by Fidelle Duvivier in 1787 is generally attributed to him, we know that his ambition to make porcelain was fulfilled. However, since he died in 1787, five years after he left New Hall, he cannot have made much porcelain. The tea-wares which have been identified in recent years as being made by Turner were almost certainly made after 1800 (their shapes are similar to those used for 'Turner's Patent' ware) and thus must have been made by his sons.[3] Although some of the patterns used are either the same as, or similar to, those used by New Hall these wares do not really resemble the New Hall shapes and should not be easily mistaken for the wares of this factory.

ANTHONY KEELING
born 1738, died 1815

Anthony Keeling was the other partner to leave the company in 1782. He had married into the potting world in 1760, when he married Ann Booth, the daughter of the famous potter Enoch Booth. Keeling evidently partnered Booth before his marriage, since on 6 December 1759 there is mention in the *Edinburgh Evening Courant* of a saleroom/warehouse business in their joint names. After Booth's death Keeling took over the Cliff Bank works at Tunstall and later built the Phoenix Works, where in 1781 the first New Hall porcelain was made. He was clearly a capable and experienced potter.

It is not known how New Hall retailed their porcelain but I am inclined to believe that they had warehouses or agents in some provincial cities. In fact it once seemed possible that one of the reasons for Keeling's presence on the board was his

[2] Illustrated in B. Hillier, op. cit., frontispiece and Plate 34b.

[3] Geoffrey Godden (editor), *Staffordshire Porcelain*, 1983, chapter 6.

warehouse in Edinburgh. However, this was not the case, for in 1775 (1 April and 18 November) newspaper notices appeared saying that he had decided to give up his business in Edinburgh, and the stock was sold. There were no further notices of a warehouse or saleroom in his name after that date although his name did appear in the street directories until 1782–3. The date 1775–6 for the closure of the Edinburgh warehouse assumes more significance if coupled with the fact that Keeling owed money (£6 3s 3d) to John Wedgwood, 'earth potter' of the Big House, Burslem, for wares supplied. Wedgwood's account book shows that during the period 1761 to 1775 Anthony Keeling bought spoons, melons and 'unfired wares' from him. It seems likely that Keeling was in some financial difficulty in 1775, hence the Edinburgh sale. Perhaps in 1782 his finances were not stable enough to continue with the New Hall Company.

After leaving the New Hall Company Keeling continued to make Queen's ware and Egyptian black until he retired to Liverpool in 1810 and died there in 1815.

The New Hall partnership embraced many religions. Samuel Hollins was a pillar of the Anglican Church, Jacob Warburton a Roman Catholic, John Daniel a Free Thinker, and Anthony Keeling was for many years the principal supporter of a place of worship on his premises, for a society of the sect of Christians called Sandemanians.[4]

JOHN HOLLINS
died 1804[5]

The name John Hollins appears on two documents which may be assumed to refer to the same man. He was probably not directly related to Samuel Hollins in spite of the fact that Samuel had a younger brother called John who lived to be ninety-six years old (1759–1855). The 'Surrender' document of 1779 already mentioned (page 14) refers to John Hollins, of Newcastle, mercer, and the 1803 'agreement' (page 13) refers to John Hollins of Newcastle-under-Lyme, gentleman. The Wedgwood archives have many accounts which were rendered by John Hollins, mercer and draper of Newcastle-under-Lyme, to Josiah Wedgwood. Josiah's family were good customers and the accounts were rendered annually. That for 1776, for instance, shows twenty-three different visits, after which 204 items of household drapes, linen or haberdashery were listed with a total value of £57 14s 2d. We can only assume

[4] Ll. Jewitt, *The Ceramic Art of Great Britain*, 1878, vol. 2, p. 303.

[5] *Staffordshire Advertiser*, 31 March 1804: 'died at his son's house at Hanley, John Hollins of Newcastle, alderman, and one of the persons in the New Hall Manufactory, a few days ago.'

that John Hollins was a financial backer who left the firm shortly after the fourteen-year lease agreement was signed in 1803.

SAMUEL HOLLINS
born 1748, died 1820

Samuel Hollins was a respected and respectable member of the community. He was the sixth son in a family of nine children and was the father of six children by his first marriage. His father's (Richard Hollins) generous help towards the building of the first St John's Church in Hanley was continued by his own philanthropy in the building of another Hanley church in 1787 and the parsonage house in 1813. Samuel Hollins's stock stood high enough in 1796 for him to become the mayor of the Mock Corporation of Hanley and Shelton. Such integrity at the head of the New Hall Company must have been of inestimable value.

Although he inherited a share in two coal mines (Birches Head Mine and Roe Hurst Mine) from his father, Samuel Hollins was a potter. His factory at Cauldon Canal, Vale Pleasant, Shelton, made cream-coloured earthenware and 'red-china'; the most frequently found products are dark-red stonewares, some of which bear the impressed mark 's. HOLLINS'. There is no connection between these pieces and those marked 'T & J HOLLINS', which were made independently by his two nephews. The production of pottery at Vale Pleasant was carried on whilst he was a member of the New Hall Company so that when he bought a 'messuage, mill and other freehold lands and hereditaments, lying within the Manor or Lordship of Bucknall', from a William Adams for £1000, the mill was probably used in the preparation of materials for both factories. Evidence for his continued interest in his own pottery is found in the numerous accounts preserved in the Wedgwood archives. As late as 1801 (12 February) Messrs Wedgwood and Co. bought 'Red China Teapots, Bowles, Sugar Boxes and Cream Ewers' to the value of £1 0s 0¾d from Samuel Hollins.

It is one of the tragedies of New Hall that there was no family continuity within the company. There was only one son amongst the six children that Hollins had by his first wife (Nancy Daintry from Leek) and he (Thomas) went to Manchester, where he was styled a merchant. There were no children from his second marriage, to Ann Sutton, and so it was to Thomas that the Hollins share in the 'New Hall China Works' (valued at £5,975) was bequeathed in 1820. On the other hand, one of his daughters, Ann, married Herbert Minton, but they had the Minton firm to work for and maintain. The final irony, so far as New Hall is concerned, is that Samuel Hollins's grandson, Michael Daintry Hollins (born 1815), although qualifying in

Manchester as a surgeon, gave up his career to become a partner in the Minton firm with his uncle Herbert.

JACOB WARBURTON
born 1741, died 1826

PETER WARBURTON
born 1773, died 1813

JOHN DANIEL
born 1756, died 1821

The *Staffordshire Advertiser* of 30 September 1826 contains this obituary notice of Jacob Warburton (probably written by Simeon Shaw):

> Forty years ago in conjunction with a few other spirited individuals, Jacob Warburton contracted with the late Richard Champion, Esq., a respectable merchant in Bristol, for the purchase of his patent right to the exclusive use of Cornish clay and stone for the manufacture of porcelain. In the year 1782, after making some experiments at Tunstall under the direction of Mr Champion, they established a china manufactory at the New Hall in Shelton. . . . Mr Warburton had for many years withdrawn himself from the cares and fatigues of his commercial engagements and on his second marriage, the result of a long cemented friendship and mutual attachment, he retired to Ford Green House. . . .

Jacob Warburton was the second son of John Warburton and Ann Daniel. John Daniel was the nephew of Ann Daniel. The two families can be considered together when studying their part in the history of New Hall. The potting traditions of the Warburton and Daniel families were long, both names being known in potting circles in the seventeenth century. At the beginning of the eighteenth century Joseph Warburton (1694–1752) was potting in Hot Lane and was considered to be one of the most important manufacturers. His son John (1720–61) married Ann Daniel, herself a master potter, who survived him by thirty-seven years. After her husband's death Ann carried on a very successful and important enamelling business with her son Thomas under the title 'Ann Warburton and Son'.

Jacob Warburton, Ann's second son, had his own pottery at Cobridge when he became one of the proprietors of the New Hall China Manufactory; he continued to run his own pottery, and Jewitt says that he succeeded his mother in the family potworks.

Simeon Shaw, the ceramic historian and chemist, knew Jacob Warburton well and wrote of him in glowing terms, mentioning also his literary and linguistic talent. Even allowing for exaggeration by Shaw we can see that the Warburton name was respected. A number of letters to Josiah Wedgwood are preserved. On 17 August 1771 he was writing for 'ten tons of clay from Northwich' and 'three tons of Baddeley clay from Winsford' that had been promised to him; he mentions also an order of 'ten table-sets' for Wedgwood. In 1771 Wedgwood asked Warburton to act as his arbitrator in his dispute with Humphrey Palmer over the latter's infringement of Wedgwood's patent for 'ornamenting earthenware and porcelain with a peculiar species of encaustic painting'. Later, in 1790, Jacob was enquiring about small jasper vases 'which are us'd in Germany at table, being fill'd with flowers'. Some time before the 1803 agreement, probably in 1800, when he retired from his own works, Jacob had retired from the New Hall partnership in favour of his son Peter and, after his second marriage in 1814, he lived at Ford Green House (now one of the City of Stoke-on-Trent museums). His second wife was Ann (née Ford) the widow of Joseph Bucknall, a potter of Cobridge.

There were seven children born of his marriage to Mary Stone of Cobridge in 1766, four boys and three girls. The youngest son, Benjamin, eventually lived in Dorset near to two of his sisters, Ann (Pike) and Catherine (Voss), who had married clay-merchants who sold ball clay to the Staffordshire potters.

Two of the sons, Peter and Francis, in partnership made good quality creamware at Bleak Hill in Cobridge. In 1802 their partnership was dissolved; Francis set up a factory at La Charité-sur-Loire (Nièvre) and Peter continued on his own. At this time Peter also took his father's place in the New Hall partnership and was involved in the buying of the estate in 1810. Peter may not have had much say in the day-to-day running of New Hall, since he continued to work his own factory, which had two kilns (a plan of the factory was attached to Jacob Warburton's will). His most important achievement was the discovery of the method of transfer-printing in gold for which he took out a patent in 1810. His death in 1813 at the age of forty was a severe blow to New Hall. Peter Warburton married Mary Emery, whose father Francis is said to have been the decorating manager at New Hall. This may be true but there is no further evidence. Jewitt refers to a Mr F. J. Emery as working for T. Furnival and Son before becoming the proprietor of the Bleak Hill works.[6] If Mr F. J. Emery was Peter Warburton's father-in-law it is possible that he became the proprietor of Bleak Hill works in 1813 on Peter's death.

John, the other son, continued to run the family potworks, which was next to Peter's, after his father retired in 1800.[7] This explains the statement in Jacob's will

[6] Ll. Jewitt, op. cit., vol. 2, p. 295.

[7] *Staffordshire Advertiser*, 22 November 1800: 'Jacob & John Warburton, potters, Cobridge, dissolving partnership – debts to be paid to Jacob; John continues; from 15 November 1800.'

that 'I have in my life time given to my son John Warburton more than an equal Share of my Effects. I do not think it right to leave him any part of my remaining property.' In 1799 John had been a cause of great consternation to his father when he set his cap at Kitty Wedgwood – Josiah's sister, who lived at Henbury near Bristol.

We turn now to John Daniel, the cousin of Jacob Warburton, who was employed as the manager of the New Hall Company after Richard Champion had left. His ability, loyalty and competence can be assessed by the fact that he was the New Hall manager for about forty years, until in 1821 he was succeeded by John Tittensor. There can be no doubt that he was in charge of the day-to-day running of the works even after he became a partner in the firm (1801 at the latest, since a letter of this date mentions Hollins, Warburton, Daniel and Co.). Many of the bills and letters in the Wedgwood archives bear his signature.[8] At a special court held on 4 August 1814 the title of the New Hall Estate was put in his name on behalf of the firm Hollins, Warburton, Daniel and Co.

The *Staffordshire Advertiser* of 27 January 1821 recorded his death thus:

> On Thursday the 18th inst., John Daniel Gent of Hanley aged 65 years, one of the proprietors of the long established concern the New Hall China Manufactory . . . his mortal remains were conveyed in a hearse (attended by a number of his friends in carriages) to Endon in this County on Wednesday last, and interred in a piece of ground at the village belonging to him . . . he was committed to the 'House appointed for all living' without the observance of the offices in religion of any shape, conformably with the opinions of the Free Thinkers to which it is understood he had long been a disciple. The singularity of the occasion collected together a multitude of spectators on the road to Endon and at the place of interment.

When his sister Alice died in 1827, she was buried in the same tomb and in her will left money for its maintenance. Alas, houses are now built on the field and the grave, which is in a private garden, has been levelled and is covered by a grass lawn.

CHARLES BAGNALL
born 1747, died 1814

Although Charles Bagnall is recorded as being a potter, and a partner to Joshua Heath, it seems likely that he acted more as a business man on the New Hall board.

[8]One is illustrated, Plate 5, p. 32.

Like Samuel Hollins, he was a respected member of the community and subscribed to the rebuilding of St John's Church. In 1784, together with other partners, he attended the first Mayor's Feast at Hanley.

On the business side, a lease of the Carloggas Pit (on Lord Camelford's land) was taken out in 1795 in the name of Bagnall and Co. This has been thought to be a pseudonym for the New Hall Company since the mine was previously leased to them when Champion's patent was procured. Then, when these agreements were reviewed, Bagnall took part in the negotiations. In 1799 he signed as a partner in the Hendra Company.[9] He was also a coalmaster, being one of the many partners in Samuel Perry and Co., who owned the New Hays and Sneyd Green collieries. In 1797 this partnership was dissolved. Adding to the diversity of his business activities, Bagnall is listed as a lead merchant in 1800. Charles Bagnall was still a partner in the firm when the partnership changes were announced in the *Staffordshire Advertiser* of 10 November 1804, but he did not continue as a partner when the estate was bought in 1810.

JOSHUA HEATH

Facts about Joshua Heath are hard to find. Certainly the name of Heath has been associated with potting since the early part of the eighteenth century. There seems little doubt that Joshua was a potter although no wares can be ascribed to him. In 1770 Joshua Heath together with many other potters signed an agreement on prices, whilst Jewitt says that Charles Bagnall was 'formerly a partner of Joshua Heath'. The list of potters in Hanley in 1787 included 'Heath, Warburton and Co, china manufacturers' but the 1803 Agreement only referred to 'Joshua Heath and Charles Bagnall of Shelton'.

WILLIAM CLOWES
born c. 1745, died 1822

William Clowes, of Longport, gentleman was named as a copartner in the 1803 Agreement, the 1804 notice in the *Staffordshire Advertiser*, the buying of the New Hall Estate in 1810; and in 1821, upon the death of John and Alice Daniel, the title of the New Hall Estate was put in his name on behalf of the firm Hollins, Warburton,

---

[9]The Hendra Company was formed by a group of Staffordshire potters to work a clay mine at Hendra Common in Cornwall, and thus obtain china-clay and -stone for their own use, and for sale to other manufacturers.

Daniel and Co. He also signed the Hendra Company agreement in 1799. At no time was he described as a potter and his name never appears in the title of the New Hall Company. I firmly believe that he gave only financial support to the firm. To understand this more readily we must consider his family background.

His father, also William, was born in 1728, married Jane Henshall (whose elder sister Ann married James Brindley, the engineer, in 1750), and died in 1782. His uncle Josiah was born in 1735 and married twice. Josiah's first wife, who was Elizabeth Bagnall (sister or aunt of a Charles Bagnall – possibly the New Hall partner) died in 1763, only seven weeks after their wedding; his second wife, Margaret, died four months after him in May 1795 and all Josiah's money and estate was inherited by his nephew William (copartner in the New Hall China Manufactory). Uncle Josiah became one of the most important canal engineers in England between 1771 and 1794, bridging the gap between James Brindley and Thomas Telford. One of his first great tasks and achievements was with the Trent and Mersey Canal. He had taken part in the sod-cutting ceremony on 26 July 1766, and when Brindley died in 1772 he assisted Hugh Henshall (the brother of Jane who married Josiah's brother William) to complete the construction of the canal. Besides going on to become a famous and successful canal constructor and engineer, he was interested in the promotion of investment in canals. He also in 1777 went into partnership with Hugh Henshall in a canal carrying company working mainly at Middlewich – the exchange port for broad barges to the narrow boats working between Preston Brook and Stoke. When he died he was a wealthy man with shares in excess of £1000 in many companies he was working for, as well as a farm at Biddulph (valued at £1000) and property in Cheshire and Staffordshire.

I cannot believe that William Clowes was immune to his home and family environment. I have always thought that the expansion of the canal system influenced the New Hall partners in their venture and I suggest that William Clowes among the partners had the real entrepreneurial spark. Whilst he may not have had so much money when the Champion patent was bought, he had inherited in 1795, long before the copyhold was bought.

William Clowes married twice. By his first wife Sarah (née Hollins) he had a son William, who died in 1816, and a daughter Elizabeth, who married William Harrison of Manchester. There were two daughters by his second wife Margaret: Ann, who married Hugh Henshall Williamson (late of Longport and then of Greenway Bank), and Sarah, who married Jacob Jones of Droitwich.

Besides his interest in the New Hall Company, William Clowes's will mentions 'also the several Mines and Veins of Coal and Slack lying under that part of the settled Estate at Whitfield which was purchased from the late John Sneyd Esquire and under other Copyhold Lands thereto adjoining which mines I heretofore purchased from John Sparrow Esquire and Mr John Hales also all my Leases, Terms and Interests in certain Mines of Coal lying under other Lands in Norton-in-the-Moors aforesaid. . . . And also my Leasehold Interest . . . in a stream of water supplying a Flint Mill erected upon my said settled Estate at Whitfield.'

His sons-in-law William Harrison and Hugh Henshall Williamson were named trustees, and the latter became the negotiator, firstly for Clowes's daughters and then for the families of the three other partners, when the New Hall Estate was finally sold to William Loftus Lowndes in 1843.

NOTE ON SOURCES USED IN CHAPTER 3

The sources for the information given in this chapter are the books by W. A. Pitt, Simeon Shaw, J. Ward, Llewellynn Jewitt, J. C. Wedgwood, G. E. Stringer, B. Hillier and R. M. Barton, the *Apollo* article by R. G. Haggar listed in the Bibliography, documents in the Wedgwood Archives in Keele University, documents and wills in the William Salt Library, Stafford, an article in *Waterways News*, and advertisements in the *Staffordshire Advertiser* and the *Edinburgh Evening Courant*.

CHAPTER 4

The New Hall China Manufactory
1781–1835

It is interesting and intriguing to speculate upon the vision of the Staffordshire potters who agreed terms with Champion. What motivated this group of men to accept a challenge which Wedgwood had avoided?

The Industrial Revolution, which was to change irrevocably the entire structure of the working world and the lives of the middle class, began long before the New Hall partners bought Richard Champion's patent. I think these potters saw the opening of a new and growing market for porcelain tea-wares. An increase in wealth and a rising standard of living took place in many families and, although they may not have been able to afford silver or the most expensive porcelain tea-services, nevertheless they may no longer have been satisfied with the common creamware. I believe that the New Hall partners foresaw a market for simple and comparatively cheap gilded and coloured tea-sets; nothing so expensive as the finest Worcester porcelain and yet more colourful than blue-and-white, more refined than earthenware.

These potters must also have been aware of the increase in the habit and custom of tea-drinking. During the eighteenth century the price of tea was gradually reduced and finally, in 1784, the tax on it was removed. Although this latter point may seem to us in this tax-ridden age to be the ultimate blessing, it has been suggested that in fact it made little difference to the quantity of tea that was consumed. So much was smuggled into the country that only the legality of its use was affected!

Since this new market was growing in the heart of England, that is the midlands and the industrial north, a convenient site for the works was obviously Staffordshire. From there trade routes would be short and the wares could be sold

1. CREAM-JUG decorated in enamels (pattern 22). This shape of jug is more commonly found made by the Caughley and Worcester factories. Height 5.5 cm (2.2 in), hard-paste, 1785–90. *See page 80.*

3. Pair of CASTORS decorated with yellow enamel and gold. Mark: N206. Height 9.1 cm (3.6 in), hard-paste, c. 1790. *See page 96.*

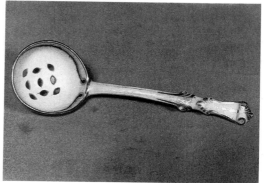

2. LADLE from a dessert-service decorated with underglaze dark-blue and gold. Length 16.5 cm (6.5 in), hard-paste, 1782–7.

4. Pierced LADLE *en suite* with that shown in Plate 2. Length 16 cm (6.3 in), hard-paste, 1782–7. *See page 96.*

easily by travellers, so that the partners might have hoped for early profitability. As it happened, within a decade news of the quality of New Hall wares had reached London. In November 1792, the manager of the Derby retail shop in London, Joseph Lygo, suggested to Richard Egan, a Bath chinaman, that he should order New Hall porcelain.[1]

Little is known about the retail outlets for the New Hall wares. Perhaps some was sold in the Derby shop in London? The 1802 bankruptcy sale[2] of the London chinaman, Joseph Tansley, included New Hall tea-wares. John Turner's wares were sold by Abbott and Mist from their warehouse in Fleet Street. I have seen a service, made probably between 1800 and 1810,[3] with a mark of 'Abbott and Mist, Fleet Street' (page 128) under the lid of both the teapot and the sucrier. It is mentioned elsewhere (page 15) that Anthony Keeling had a warehouse in Edinburgh, but it was closed before New Hall began. On the other hand, some tea-sets have been noted which bore the marks 'Cotton, High Street, Edinburgh' and 'E. Cotton, Edinburgh' (page 128). It would appear that these sets were sold by Elijah Cotton, who had a 'stone, glass and china warehouse' in High Street, Edinburgh, about 1806–10. In the 1820s the Herculaneum warehouse in Duke Street, Liverpool, purchased large quantities of New Hall; obviously this was for retail or export.

The exact location of a factory was very important for commercial success, as Champion pointed out in his 1781 'Address to the Pottery'.[4] Primarily it needed to have both raw materials at hand and good transport facilities. The existing porcelain makers like Caughley, Lowestoft and Worcester were well served by water-borne transport which enabled them safely to import their materials and export their wares. Clay and coal occur abundantly in Staffordshire and to the potter local coal is the more useful. At first sight this may seem unlikely, but it is true. Although a simple piece of underglaze blue-and-white porcelain may receive only two firings (about forty-eight hours for the biscuit and fourteen hours for the glaze) it is possible for a finely decorated piece of porcelain to be fired six times. In making one ton of finished ware a potter might use ten to twelve tons of coal. Thus many of the

[1] The letters of Joseph Lygo to William Duesbury, father and son, are at the Derby Local Studies Library, a part of the Central Library, Derby.

[2] 'A Catalogue of the extensive Stock in Trade of Mr Joseph Tansley a Bankrupt – Great Mary Le Bone Street – comprising a general assortment of Porcelain, Glass and Earthenware.' Sold by Mr Phillips on 12 January 1802.

[3] The service has a large-size boat-shaped teapot and is decorated with on-glaze bat-prints in black, pattern 709.

[4] Appendix I, 2, pp. 223–6.

Staffordshire potbanks were built beside a coal mine rather than a clay pit.

In the second half of the eighteenth century transport throughout the country improved. In 1762, when a petition was presented to Parliament, the conditions described were appalling. Clay and stone from Cornwall and Dorset could be carried by barge either on the Rivers Mersey and Weaver to Winsford in Cheshire or up the River Trent from Hull to Willington in Derbyshire. A pack horse or carriage had to be used for the remainder of the journey (about sixteen miles from Winsford and about thirty miles from Willington). No wonder there was agitation for turnpike roads. Yet when these were made they were not sufficient to cope with the developing industry. In 1777, the water link between the Trent and Mersey (named originally the Grand Trunk Canal) was opened and from that year the real industrial importance and prosperity of Staffordshire grew. At last supplies of raw materials could be easily and cheaply transported;[5] the fragile final product could be carried gently and safely. No doubt the triumphant success of the Grand Trunk Canal was a major factor both in Champion's decision to turn to the Potteries for help, and in the acceptance by our group of potters of the challenge which their vision presented.

This canal enabled Staffordshire potters to increase their exports, which even in 1765, before its construction, exceeded the home consumption. North America, France, Holland, Sweden and Germany were all good markets. Unfortunately, as the proportion of exports rose the ceramic industry began to suffer from the effects of international squabbles, with their spiteful blockades and retaliatory import duties. Balance of payments problems and protection were as real in the eighteenth century as they are today.

It is not known whether the New Hall partners considered building up an export trade. Whether they did or not, their early years must have been affected by the American War, which caused much distress in Staffordshire. In fact the hard times and recessions in trade caused by this war must have increased the problems of the newly-born company. In 1783 rioting occurred at Etruria and troops had to be called out to restore order.

America was not the only export market. Europe was a closer neighbour and the earthenware manufacturers strove to sell their products across the Channel. There were high tariffs to contend with, barriers which the superior quality of the Staffordshire creamware was able to surmount. Some of these barriers, especially those in France and Germany, had been raised in response to similar action by

[5]J. C. Wedgwood, in *Staffordshire Pottery and its History*, 1913, writes that only nine years after the canal was opened, the freight for general goods was 1¼d per ton per mile, or less than one-seventh of the cost before the canal was cut.

England against the importation of European porcelain. A commercial treaty with France was signed in 1786 which once more opened the doors for trade. Staffordshire seems to have benefited very much from this treaty and we must remember that Josiah Wedgwood played a part in putting forward the potters' views to the authorities. Trade boomed and the value of exports rose.

The French wars, which lasted on and off until 1815, had comparatively little effect upon the Staffordshire potters until 1806, when Napoleon issued from Berlin his famous decrees declaring the British Isles to be in a state of blockade. Unfortunately American ships became involved in the retaliatory English blockade and they too closed their ports to English goods. Between 1806 and 1812 the export trade declined seriously and many potters became bankrupt. The New Hall partners must have had great courage to buy their lease in 1810 and then, between 1812 and 1814, change over from their proven hard-paste to the new bone-china body.

Probably the nadir was reached in 1812. A slight improvement in trade followed until peace came with France and Napoleon finally beaten. Peace and the cumulative effects of the Industrial Revolution hoisted Great Britain in 1815 to the brink of an unprecedented period of greatness and prosperity. Alas, this greatness did not mean eternal industrial prosperity. The immediate boom was short-lived and followed by economic crisis. Thereafter it was a case of fluctuating recovery.

The problems of transport and supply of raw materials had been largely solved by the turn of the century, but labour difficulties and low wages caused increasing unrest; the cost of living had risen but the level of wages had not. As articulate leaders came forward workers became united and although they were beaten in their first efforts to strike in 1825, the time was soon to come when they were not to be quelled. The ten years from 1830 was a period of great unrest and strife in Staffordshire.

The life of New Hall must be seen within this economic picture, largely determined by international politics. Its porcelain was probably made for the home market, though since it was a part of a close-knit community whose products were exported widely, complete independence was impossible. To a certain extent the effects of both good times and bad must have been diffused from one factory to another. The potteries were not enjoying prosperity when the group of potters started their trials at Anthony Keeling's factory in 1781. These trials did not last long because in 1782 Champion left to go to America, and the potters disagreed amongst themselves. We know nothing about this disagreement but the outcome was that Turner and Keeling left and a new factory site was found.

Recent study of copyhold leases of Shelton Hall has elicited some interesting information, although as is so often the case, there are some tantalising missing pieces in the puzzle. Shelton Hall and its extensive outbuildings must have been used by potters for some considerable time before our story begins. In 1773 Alice Dalton, the widow of Edward Dalton of Litchfield, surrendered the copyhold of the Shelton Hall Estate to Humphrey Palmer of the Churchyard Works, Hanley. Humphrey Palmer was a well-known potter who after 1778 went into partnership with James Neale. He caused Josiah Wedgwood a lot of trouble by imitating his wares and using his patented process for encaustic decoration of pottery. Humphrey Palmer did not work at Shelton Hall, since the potworks was at that time in the holding of Samuel Boulton.

In 1777 Palmer, about to re-marry, settled the copyhold after his demise upon Hannah Ashwin, his bride-to-be, and any children they might have. At this time the premises were still let, but to a different tenant, his son Thomas Palmer. The annual rent was £30 and the lease mentions 'Shelton Hall with the Pot Ovens, Potworks – stables etc.'.[6]

The next recorded surrender document (see page 14) has been lost, but it gave valuable information. It showed that in 1779 Thomas Palmer had already yielded the tenancy to Ralph Baddeley of Shelton, and that he was handing it over to John Turner. Since no one seemed to settle in this potworks, one wonders why Turner was interested. Was it leased with a speculative eye for a successful outcome of the research association convened by Wedgwood, or had he some prior knowledge of Champion's plans? When he left the New Hall partners we must presume that he either sublet or surrendered his lease to them. It is unfortunate that these important documents are missing and unrecorded. In fact, the New Hall partners are not mentioned in the copyhold leases until 1802, although Humphrey Palmer had died in 1789 and his daughter Mary had inherited the copyhold of Shelton Hall.

Shelton Hall was well situated for materials and transport. There were several wharves and warehouses on the Grand Trunk Canal and from one of these, Etruria wharf, a horse railway ran up to the centre of Hanley. Although this did not run directly to the Hall, any journey from it would probably have been on the level or even slightly downhill. By this means clay and stone could be carried. Coal may have been mined on the estate, since there is a clause in the lease[7] about subsidence damage caused by coal mining and Mr Stringer records finding a pit shaft beneath the floor of one of the buildings.[8] When the site was excavated recently to enable a supermarket to be built, there was ample evidence of coal in the ground.

[6]Appendix II, –/1/2, 4 September 1777, p. 232.

[7]Appendix II, –/1/5, 1 March 1803, p. 232–3.

[8]G. E. Stringer, *New Hall Porcelain*, 1949, p. 57.

Furthermore, the coal mines owned by Samuel Hollins, Charles Bagnall and William Clowes, which were not far away, might have supplied the factory with coal.

The cost of china-clay and china-stone had always been a thorn in Champion's flesh, especially when he tried to sell the patent. Despite the facility with which other potters seemed able to buy these raw materials more cheaply, New Hall were probably forced to take over Champion's lease from Lord Camelford. There were conditions attached to this lease for both sides. Lord Camelford was not to sell the materials to any other potters, whilst the lessees would be considered to default if they left the rent unpaid for sixty days or failed to work the pit for two years. It is clear that New Hall did not comply fully, since in 1789 Lord Camelford sought legal advice on unpaid rent and apparent neglect of the mines. Although Camelford was unable to foreclose, the legal enquiries stirred the lessees, who restarted mining operations – perhaps under a revised agreement. In 1795 after further investigations the lease was granted to Bagnall and Co. (i.e. New Hall) until 1796, when the patent expired and a junior Lord Camelford, who succeeded to the title in 1793, came of age. Once the patent had expired, competition in buying china-clay and china-stone must have increased, and New Hall probably felt that they had greater freedom in choosing their source of materials. In 1799 they took out a lease on Hendra Common and almost immediately, with Thomas Minton, took a leading part in the formation of the Hendra Company. This company, which also included Wedgwood and Adams, continued as an effective supplier of materials until well into the nineteenth century. It did not fail until about 1839.

Ball-clay, so named because it was sold in large balls, was used by the potters as well as china-clay. Although less pure than the china-clay, it restores to a mixture some of the strength and plasticity which has been refined out of the kaolin. Staffordshire potters had been importing it from Dorset since the 1760s. Josiah Wedgwood and Ralph Baddeley in 1771, for instance, concluded an agreement for 1,700 tons of clay a year for twenty-one years. Samuel Hollins (presumably for the New Hall Company) joined many other Staffordshire potters in 1791 in making an agreement with William Pike for 1,200 tons of ball-clay for five years. William Pike's family originated in Chudleigh in Devon before moving to Corfe Castle. It is interesting to speculate whether this agreement led to the introduction of Jacob Warburton's daughter Ann to her future husband. She married William Pike on 18 August 1803 at the parish church in Norton-in-the-Moors, in Staffordshire (in which churchyard are buried Jacob Warburton and William Clowes). The trustees for Jacob Warburton's will were William Pike, William Voss and his own son Benjamin, all of the parish of Church Knowle in the County of Dorset. Presumably Benjamin worked with the clay-merchants in Dorset.

Once the clays and stone arrived in Shelton they had to be prepared for use. The traditional powers, wind and water, were used for mills when the factory started but steam power was soon to be introduced to the Potteries. Boulton's Sun and Planet engines were installed by Josiah Wedgwood at Etruria in 1784 and 1793 and later by other manufacturers. In New Hall's early years grinding was probably done in the Bucknall mills which Samuel Hollins bought in 1788. Bagnall's lease on the Sneyd Mills in 1792 would help to increase the output of prepared materials, some of which New Hall sold to other potters. These two mills were nominally owned by individual members of the New Hall Company; in 1806, however, the company itself enlarged its estate by buying some adjacent land and water. On this they built a mill and thus gained independence. Here steam power was used, for the 1831 New Hall sale advertisement (page 38) mentioned 'the steam engine mill at Booden Brook'.

There has been much speculation about the prepared materials which New Hall sold to other potters. The name 'composition' was mentioned by several nineteenth-century ceramic writers, a word which I believe means a mixture which could be used as a basis for a glaze. Evidence can be found in the Wedgwood Commonplace Book 1786–1794, which was compiled by Alexander Chisholm, Wedgwood's chemist from 1780 to 1795. On page 67, he quotes from 'the late George Barnett's pocket book, April 23, 1789':

> *The Newhall composition*
> 2 of moorstone⎫
> 1 of flint　　⎭ ground fine together at the mill.
> *Common cream colour glaze for a blending*
> 40 pounds Newhall composition⎫
> 65½ do. White Lead　　　　　⎭ Sift them for use
> *Composition for a Blue Glaze*
> 12 pounds More stone, 6 flint, 22 white lead
> *A China Glaze* . . . when from the mill, mix it with a common composition 1 to 7, that is, 1 of the fine glaze to 7 of the composition. Then sift for use.
> Observe that the common composition is mixed 1 flint and 2 moorstone, and then 40 lbs of this mixture to 65½ pounds of white lead for a blending.

In spite of the difficult trading conditions of 1783 the first products of the factory were excellent and undoubtedly found a market. A large variety of wares were made which were decorated with restrained gilt decoration for 'Sunday best', as well as attractive, neat polychrome patterns. An invoice from New Hall to Josiah

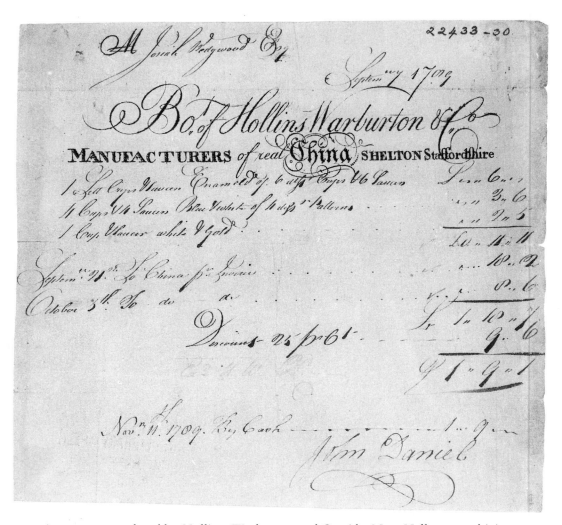

5.   An account rendered by Hollins, Warburton and Co. (the New Hall partnership) to
     Josiah Wedgwood Esq. and dated 7 September 1789. *Josiah Wedgwood and Sons Ltd.,
     Barlaston.*

Wedgwood gives an idea of the contemporary prices and the relative importance of
the different styles of decoration. The invoice shows that one cup and saucer cost
10½d if the decoration was blue-and-white, but 1s when enamelled and 2s 5d gilded.
A number of letters and accounts besides this one are among the Wedgwood
manuscripts. These give a fascinating picture of the interchanges between local
potters at this time. Just as Wedgwood bought porcelain from New Hall for his

customers, so John Daniel bought red teapots from Thomas Wedgwood in 1777 and 1778 and also supplied wares which Mr Boardman transported for him. Wedgwood was asked to pack a New Hall saucer for a customer. In 1790 and 1801 New Hall were caught short of gold and asked the favour of a short loan from Mr Byerley at Wedgwood's, and in 1806, when James Cookson was in the New Hall office, they supplied some colours to Messrs Wedgwood and Byerley's Mills. In 1812 the billhead proclaimed that the firm was 'Hollins, Warburton, Daniel & Co., Manufacturers of Real China', and New Hall supplied Wedgwood with teacups, saucers and bread-plates decorated with pattern 446. The last two letters express an apology for not settling an account quickly, followed by overpayment and a request to 'hand the difference to the bearer'.

About 1790 the wide range of products was rationalised and soon a standard range of tea-sets was sold. The quality of decoration also became generally more pedestrian. The release in 1790 of their chief decorator, Duvivier, is clearly related to this change of policy (see page 120). Nevertheless, although the wares were of a mundane quality they found a ready market. The paste and glaze were consistent and gradually improved so that the potting and translucency reached a good standard. Gas bubbles always filled the glaze but the pools of surplus glaze became shallower. The style of decoration changed and – some think – deteriorated. No doubt it reflected contemporary taste and fashion. For the same reason tea-bowls gave way to teacups about 1800.

Insurance policies[9] taken out with the Salop Fire Office in 1792, 1793 and 1810 give some indication of the changing use of buildings. From the first one, dated 22 March 1792, we can deduce that they had so much stock, both china and biscuit, that it could not be stored in the buildings at New Hall alone but that a further store in a potworks at Booden Brook was needed. I do not think that there is any suggestion that the pots were being made at Booden Brook, for there is mention of neither biscuit-ware nor working utensils in the policy. Whilst it is probable that the New Hall Estate extended to the Booden Brook there is no indication that this potworks was on their land. Alice Daniel's will indicates that she owned land at Booden Brook and that the New Hall Fire Engine Mill had been erected on land bought from her. It is possible that the potworks referred to here is the one recorded in 1802 as being run by Hewitt and Buckley. A second policy, dated 13 April 1793, tells us that the main store at Hanley had been moved to new buildings and the stock from Booden Brook had been brought to the 'New Hall'. This must have been the year when the Hall was converted from a 'dwelling house' to a 'China Warehouse'. The policy of 1810

[9]Appendix III, pp. 235–7.

names the firm as 'Messrs Hollins, Warburton, Daniel and Clowes' and for the first time includes the buildings in the schedule. Both these facts are the consequence of buying the New Hall Estate. It was apparently not the custom to insure a building unless you owned it, only the contents.

It is hard to decide who was the instigator of the fourteen-year lease agreement which was signed in 1803.[10] It is an interesting document which involves 'all that building and tenement called the New Hall formerly used and occupied as a dwelling House but now converted and used as a China Warehouse together with the Hovels, Workshops, Manufactory and Buildings belonging thereto' being let 'for the term of fourteen years' for an annual rent of £210. The firm was obviously firmly established and making tea-wares for a ready market. There was an option for either party to terminate the lease after seven years. As it happened, this option clause had to be invoked because Mary Palmer died in December 1805. The existence of this fourteen-year lease sheds new light upon the reasons for the New Hall partners' buying the copyhold in 1810. Action was forced upon them; with the death of Mary Palmer the copyhold lease had to be sold.

Seven co-partners had signed the 1803 lease: Samuel Hollins, Peter Warburton, John Daniel, John Hollins, Charles Bagnall, Joshua Heath, and William Clowes. An announcement in the *Staffordshire Advertiser* of 10 November 1804 indicated that the original contract had expired and that John Hollins and Joshua Heath had dropped out to leave five remaining partners.[11] When the whole estate was bought in 1810 Charles Bagnall had left; there were now only four partners – three potters, Hollins, Warburton and Daniel and a financial backer, William Clowes. On 16 April 1810 these four men paid £6,800 for the factory, business and estate. This important act showed courage and confidence. Economically the country was suffering the strain of war, but in the Potteries several firms like Davenport, Minton and Spode were developing confidently. However, the partners were obviously not concerned merely with their pots, they also had ideas for developing the land. The building of the Hope Congregational Church in 1812 on land next door to the factory is perhaps an indication of this, and confirmation is found in the following advertisement in the *Staffordshire Advertiser* for 7 May 1814:

---

[10]Appendix II, –/1/5, 1 March 1803, p. 33.

[11]   'NOTICE

The Partnership term lately subsisting of and in the New Hall China Manufactory, at Shelton, in the parish of Stoke upon Trent, in the county of Stafford, having expired, the said Manufactory is now carried on at New Hall aforesaid, by Messrs HOLLINS, WARBURTON, DANIEL, BAGNALL AND CLOWES, only.
Shelton 8th Nov. 1804.'

BUILDING LAND TO BE SOLD

The intended new Roads from Hanley and Shelton, in the Staffordshire Potteries being now marked out through the New Hall Estate, the public may be accommodated with Building Land in small or large lots to suit the purchaser.

For particulars apply to the Counting House, New Hall, Shelton.
NB Every liberal accommodation with respect to the time of payment will be given to purchasers of a quarter of an acre or upwards.

Much urban development was being planned at that time. In 1815, most appropriately, the Act for making Waterloo Road between Burslem and Cobridge was obtained. I believe that this road joined the two roads mentioned in the advertisement. Obviously the New Hall partners were anxious to take commercial advantage of the situation if they could.

The rise of other porcelain makers stimulated New Hall to maintain their standards and also to move with the times. The white bone-china body established by Spode was used by other potters and must have made the hard-paste porcelain look dull and lifeless by comparison. Although New Hall were forced no doubt to abandon the hard-paste they had pioneered, they achieved the change-over without either apparent deterioration in standard of product or loss of sales momentum. The date for this change-over was probably between 1812 and 1814.

The events of the next few years were critical to the New Hall Company: the decline and fall was, I believe, inevitable. If one looks at the names of the successful pottery and porcelain manufacturers it will be seen that they all have a consecutive tradition of individual leadership. Many, like Wedgwood, are from successive generations of one family. New Hall failed in this respect. A joint stock company always has difficulty when a member dies. Unless a relative can carry on, either the remaining partners or an outsider must find the money to buy the vacant share. In the latter case a real leader seems unlikely to appear; such a man would surely venture on his own.

Two of the original partners had sons, but only one of these boys had anything to do with the business and showed the promise which could have led New Hall into the future. Peter Warburton, Jacob's son, was clever. In 1810 he perfected a new method of gold-printed decoration and took out a patent for the process. In 1803 he became a partner in place of his father, who obviously wanted to retire (he was sixty-two). It was a tragedy that Peter Warburton died in 1813, predeceasing his father by thirteen years. This may have been the knell of doom for New Hall.

On 25 March 1820, in the *Staffordshire Advertiser*, the whole works were for sale in the following terms:

> China Manufactory to be disposed of by private contract and entered upon at Martinmas next, or at an earlier period if more desirable to the purchaser. That well-known and old established China Concern which has for a considerable length of time been carried on to great advantage at Newhall in the Staffordshire Potteries, under the firm of Hollins, Warburton, Daniel & Co. Any person of respectability, possessing property, wishing to embark in the China Trade, will be treated with on liberal terms. For particulars, refer to Mr Daniel, at the Manufactory, any Thursday morning.
>
> NB The stock of China, working utensils and materials to be taken at valuation for which a reasonable time will be allowed (by giving security) for payment of the same by instalment. A quantity of land to be sold to build upon, either by the yard or acre. (One concern).

This notice was repeated on 1, 8 and 15 of April but nobody came forward. It is not really surprising that the manufactory was for sale since the four partners were now old men (Samuel Hollins was seventy-two, Jacob Warburton was seventy-nine, William Clowes was sixty-six and the manager John Daniel was sixty-four). Furthermore, it would seem that John Daniel was unwell. The advertisement implies that he was attending the factory only on Thursday mornings and a codicil to Samuel Hollins' will, dated 27 April 1820, relieved Daniel from any responsibilities as a trustee or executor.

John Daniel died in 1821, the year after Samuel Hollins and two years before William Clowes. Their relatives retained their share of the firm's capital and a new manager, John Tittensor, was employed. Tittensor had been a partner in a small Hanley potworks for a short time (1803–7) before joining New Hall as a traveller in 1815. The testimony to his success was his appointment as manager, a position which he held until the factory closed in 1835.

In the *Staffordshire Advertiser* dated 3 September 1825 (and also on 10, 17 and 24) the following advertisement appeared:

> Shelton in the Potteries.
> To be sold by auction.
> By Mr James
>
> At the Swan Inn, in Hanley in the Potteries, on Thursday the 6th and

Friday the 7th days of October 1825; (the sale to commence at four o'clock in the afternoon of each day) subject to such conditions as will then be produced:

The New Hall China Works, and lands adjoining, situate in Shelton aforesaid, the whole being copyhold of inheritance within the manor of Newcastle-under-Lyme, and which will be put up in the following, or such other lots, as may be pointed out at the time of the sale.

(First Day's Sale) Thursday, 6th October 1825

Superficial Yards

Lot 1 – To consist of the long established China Works, called the New Hall (but without the range of buildings, which stand separate, fronting New Hall Street) with such of the adjoining land as is allotted to the same, the whole containing   5570

Also a valuable Steam Engine Mill at Booden Brook, in a compleat state of work, with a dwelling-house, garden and yard, as now marked out, containing in the whole   5357

Lot 2 – The said range of buildings, consisting of a dwellinghouse, and warehouses, with the land allotted thereto, extending up to New Hall Street, and containing together   1800

This lot is well adapted for the site of a Theatre, or for public offices, or for an Inn, being on the coach line of thoroughfare through the Potteries.

Lots 3 to 28 – plots of land.[12]

(Second Day's Sale) Friday, 7th October 1825

Lots 29 to 45 – plots of land.[12]

The Manufactory and Mill may be entered upon at Martinmas next, and present an opportunity that rarely occurs, of commencing business at once on a considerable scale.

A plan . . . may be seen by applying to Mr John Tittensor at the New Hall Manufactory, who will attend with the parties upon the premises. Information respecting the above may be also obtained from H. H. Williamson Esq., Greenway Bank, Mr D. G. Hales, Surveyor, Cobridge, or at the Office of Messrs Tomlinson, Solicitors, in the Potteries.

[12]Details of the plots of land have been omitted.

Once more it would seem that there were no buyers and the factory continued to make porcelain. Many of the bone-china products are of excellent quality; evidently the factory was able to maintain its standards and withstand competition. Its name was still respected since in 1830 (6 March) the name 'Hollins, Warburton, Daniel and Company' was amongst those appended to a petition denouncing 'truck' published in the *Staffordshire Advertiser*. The signatories proudly claimed that they paid their wages in money and not in bills of credit which could be redeemed only in certain shops, usually connected with the owner of the potbank. This was an insidious way of achieving a double profit.

The end of New Hall was now in sight. On Saturday, 5 March 1831, the following advertisement appeared in the *Staffordshire Advertiser*:

STAFFORDSHIRE POTTERIES.
EXTENSIVE CHINA-WORKS, STEAM ENGINE, FLINT MILL AND VALUABLE LAND FOR BUILDING PURPOSES.
TO BE SOLD BY AUCTION,
BY MR R. JOHNSON.

At the Swan Inn, in HANLEY, *in the county of Stafford, on Thursday the 24th day of March, 1831, at four o'clock in the afternoon, either altogether or in the following lots, namely:*

LOT 1. ALL that long established CHINA WORK, called the NEW HALL, situate in SHELTON, in the Staffordshire Potteries, comprising the Warehouses and plot of Land fronting to New Hall Street, and the Dwelling-house adjoining in the occupation of Mr John Tittensor, together with the Workshops, Buildings and Yards, and every requisite convenience for carrying on a most extensive business, the whole including an area, of about 7,200 superficial yards.

This lot is bounded on the south side by New Hall Street, and on the west by Brook Street, and has a communication with Hope Street on the east. In addition to its great extent, from its central situation on the main line of thoroughfare through the Potteries, it possesses local advantages for business, which can scarcely be equalled.

LOT 2 – All that STEAM ENGINE MILL, with the valuable machinery and apparatus belonging thereto, used for the grinding of flint and potter's materials, situate at Booden Brook, in Shelton aforesaid, and in the holding of Mr Thomas Crockett, together with the dwelling-house, garden and yard adjoining, the whole containing about 6,715 superficial yards of Land.

LOT 3 – The several parcels of Land lying between Great York Street, and Booden Brook and Brook Street aforesaid, and on the east side of Great York Street, contiguous to lot 1, and also on the east side of Hope Street, fronting to certain New Streets already marked or laid out, and named *Peers Street, Union Street, Cross Street, Trafalgar Row, Paddock Street.* and *Brian's Wood Street*: the whole comprising 13A. 1R. 3p. of LAND, presenting a variety of the most eligible situations for building purposes.

Also, sundry BUILDINGS, consisting of a Dwelling-House, Barn, Stable and Hovel, with the Yard about the same, situate on the south west side of Brook Street, and containing about 448 superficial yards, which will form part of lot 3.

The above property is all copyhold of inheritance of the manor of Newcastle-under-Lyme.

A plan of the premises, shewing the boundaries of the several pieces of Land comprised in Lot 3, and the lines of the different streets intersecting the same, may be seen on application to MR JOHN TITTENSOR, at the New Hall Manufactory, who will attend with parties upon the premises.

Further information may be obtained of MR LEWIS GEORGE HALES, Land Surveyor, Cobridge, or at the office of Messrs TOMLINSON, Solicitors, Cliff-Ville.

2nd March, 1831.

It would seem that there were no buyers since in the following year the *Staffordshire Advertiser* of 25 August and 1 September had this advertisement:

TO BE LET.

THAT old-established CHINA MANUFACTORY, called NEW HALL, situate in Shelton, with or without about fourteen acres of Land. The premises are in an excellent situation, and of considerable magnitude, and capable of doing an extensive business. Possession to be given at the convenience of the coming-in Tenant. – For particulars, apply to MR JOHN TITTENSOR, on the premises.

R. G. Haggar, the eminent Staffordshire ceramic historian, has suggested the possibility that Francis and Nicholas Dillon, earthenware manufacturers, were involved in the New Hall affairs and possibly had control of the works.[13] This would explain why an announcement in the *Staffordshire Advertiser* for 24 November 1832 asked for creditors of the previous Dillon partnerships to submit any outstanding accounts to John Tittensor at the New Hall Works for scrutiny.

Trade was not very good at this time and, as has been shown, there was considerable unrest among the labour force. They had been beaten when they struck in 1825 but now Robert Owen, the socialist, was preaching about the success achieved elsewhere. A new trade union (the first was in 1824) was formed and a strike in 1834 was successful. It is unlikely that the New Hall factory, having been for sale in 1820, 1825 and 1831 and to be let in 1832, even attempted to cope with these conditions and the announcement of 5 September 1835 in the *Staffordshire Advertiser* comes as no surprise:

NEW HALL MANUFACTORY, SHELTON, POTTERIES

EXTENSIVE SALE OF VALUABLE CHINA.

DEALERS and others are respectfully informed, that MR MAINWARING is instructed to Sell the whole of this superb, useful, and valuable STOCK,

BY AUCTION, without reserve;

The Company of Proprietors having concluded on retiring from trade.
Further particulars will appear in future advertisements and handbills.

Three weeks later, on 26 September, a more detailed advertisement appeared:

NEW HALL CHINA MANUFACTORY, SHELTON

VALUABLE & EXTENSIVE STOCK OF BURNISHED
GOLD CHINA.
TO BE SOLD BY AUCTION,
BY MR JOHNSON,

On the premises, at the New Hall China Manufactory, at Shelton in the Staffordshire Potteries, on Monday, Tuesday, Wednesday, Thursday, and Friday, the 5th, 6th, 7th, 8th, and 9th days of October, 1835, and the following week, (if necessary);

ALL the very valuable Stock of Burnished Gold and other CHINA, which consists of complete rich burnished gold tea services, in a great variety of shapes and patterns; also breakfast services to correspond. A very choice

---

[13] *Apollo*, vol. LIV, 1951, p. 133.

assortment of dessert and toilet services, with numerous modern and fancy-shaped jugs and mugs, chimney ornaments, &c. &c. A very general assortment of Common, China, Hawkers' Sets, &c.

This will be found a most advantageous opportunity for Merchants and China Dealers, who may rely upon every liberality being exercised towards their interest as purchasers to sell again. Likewise Inn-Keepers and the public in general, who are desirous of supplying themselves with a small assortment for their own use will find this Sale well deserving their attention.

The New Hall Company are declining business, and have let the premises, which they now occupy, with immediate possession; a circumstance which makes it quite necessary that they should dispose of their Stock without reserve.

The sale will commence each morning at eleven o'clock.

The new occupants of the premises could not have been much good or lasted long, since six years later, in 1841, John Boyle – a former partner of Herbert Minton – recorded that he had 'looked over the New Hall manuf. and found all the places in bad repair to such an extent indeed that I do not consider it tenantable in its present state. The ovens also are too large for the Hovels and all the saggar houses are small and inconvenient.'

In 1843 Hugh Henshall Williamson acting on behalf of the families of the original partners negotiated the sale of the factory, buildings, and remaining estate to William Loftus Lowndes, one of Her Majesty's Counsel in Law, for £3,050. When Lowndes died in 1865 the copyhold was bequeathed to his widow Alice, of 48 Westbourne Terrace, London and it was enfranchised in 1869. There were a number of tenants during this time: William and Thomas Hackwood in 1843, following W. Ratcliffe, had a fourteen-year tenancy at a rent of £225 per annum, and they were followed by Messrs Cockson and Harding, the forerunners of W. and J. Harding. The lease to Hackwood is an important and interesting document since it gives us a precise idea of the extent of the works premises. They leased 'that capital Earthenware Manufactory called the New Hall Manufactory consisting of five Hovels, three Sliphouses and two hardening hovels together with all and singular the warehouses, Workshops, Machine House, and other buildings and erections thereto also with the Marl Bank Clay yards'. Part of the inventory is quoted in Appendix II (page 234).

Thus the New Hall China Manufactory, which opened as a brave venture in 1781, closed without acclaim in 1835. Some of its products can be compared with the best porcelain from other factories but much was quite ordinary. The changes in shape and decoration reflect the changes in contemporary public taste and habit. A comprehensive collection of New Hall porcelain is not merely a record of the output of this small group of Staffordshire potters, it is also a social document, a vignette in which may be seen the changing aesthetic taste of the new industrial society.

CHAPTER 5

The Paste and Glaze

Did New Hall really make hard-paste porcelain? How often this question is asked! The simple answer is yes, but the explanation is more complicated.

Superficially there is no problem. It has been shown that New Hall bought Champion's patent rights and we know that they styled themselves 'Manufacturers of real porcelain' in some of their invoices, and yet the appearance of their porcelain is visibly different from the Chinese, Continental and Plymouth/Bristol products. However, this difference can be explained and does not invalidate the claim that New Hall made hard-paste porcelain. We enter the field of semantics and the definition of the words we use. After a while the words of Humpty Dumpty in *Alice Through the Looking Glass* seem strangely appropriate: 'When I use a word, it means just what I choose it to mean – neither more nor less.'

Firstly, the terms soft- and hard-paste must be defined. Most definitions quote the raw material composition and include the process by which the ingredients were used. This latter point is an important issue and is responsible for the confusion about the kind of porcelain which was made by the New Hall China Manufactory.

Fundamentally the difference between hard- and soft-paste porcelain lies in the materials which are mixed so that, when fired to a high enough temperature, a common clay is transmuted to a translucent porcelain. True or hard-paste porcelain was first made by the Chinese, and potters in other countries tried to emulate their achievement. In England, William Cookworthy was the first to find both growan- or china-stone (the Chinese call it petuntse) and china-clay (kaolin) and when he was able to use them to make porcelain, he obtained patent protection. Until this patent expired all other English porcelain makers, unless working illegally or under licence, must have made what is called artificial or soft-paste porcelain. The early artificial or soft-paste porcelains which were made at Chelsea, Derby and Longton Hall used glass in their composition to give the clay its translucency; Bow and Lowestoft added ox-bone ash as well. At Liverpool, Worcester[1] and Caughley steatite, or soapstone, was used instead of the china-clay (this is not as dramatic a difference as it sounds; china-clay is potassium aluminium silicate and soapstone is magnesium aluminium silicate). These artificial bodies, especially those made at Bow, Chelsea and Derby are physically softer than the Chinese porcelain and thus the term soft-paste is used.[2]

It seems to be a natural consequence for collectors to attempt to distinguish between the two kinds of porcelain by using a file on the footrim of the piece. This practice can only be deprecated; not only can the answer be misleading but the test piece is defaced. The physical hardness of a piece can depend upon the temperature at which it was formed as well as upon its composition. With some mixtures the higher the manufacturing temperature, the harder the product becomes. Besides, some parts of a kiln could produce better results than others: there was skill in placing the saggars[3] in a kiln.

Although close and careful examination of a piece can give some clues to its composition, the only certain way in which hard- and soft-paste can be differentiated is by chemical analysis. Even here there are problems and the results must be interpreted carefully. G. E. Stringer quotes two analyses: one done by Eccles and Rackham in 1922, and one which he had done by Dr H. W. Webb. In discussing these analyses Mr Stringer only compares them with each other whereas they must be considered alongside the analyses of glassy, soapstone and china-stone bodies. From the figures quoted in the Table on page 45 it is obvious that the alumina and silica content of the Chinese and Bristol hard-paste bodies are very similar and quite different from those of other factories. The two New Hall analyses show clearly that their body is hard-paste.

Soft-paste porcelain was made in two distinct firing stages. In the first, the biscuit stage, the shaped clay was fired at about 1,100–1,200°C, when it became translucent. Then this biscuit, as it is called, after being dipped in glaze, was fired

---

[1]A Dr Wall recipe contained 'Soapstone from Cornwall, ballclay from Barnstaple and sand from the Isle of White' (private communication from Henry Sandon in his capacity as the curator of the Dyson Perrins Museum, Worcester).

[2]Soft-paste is actually a translation of the French *pâte tendre*.

[3]A saggar is a protective box made from fired clay in which the newly-made articles were placed for firing. It protected these articles from excessive local heat of the fire.

RESULTS OF THE ANALYSIS OF PORCELAIN SPECIMENS MADE BY DIFFERENT FACTORIES

FACTORY	CHELSEA	LONGTON HALL	BOW	LOWESTOFT	DERBY	WORCESTER	CAUGHLEY	CHINESE	BRISTOL	NEW HALL	NEW HALL*	CHAMBERLAIN
Silica	64·76	76·16	43·58	41·42	41·94	72·80	74·22	71·82	69·96	73·56	68·37	75·36
Alumina	6·00	4·30	8·36	9·62	15·97	6·90	8·50	23·04	24·43	19·30	23·54	18·87
Lime	25·00	9·28	24·47	25·40	24·28	4·00	2·78	0·63	1·50	4·02	1·16	2·81
Phosphoric Acid	0·23	nil	18·95	18·77	14·96	—	0·20	0·19	0·17	0·24	0·40	0·16
Magnesia	trace	nil	0·60	—	0·20	11·85	7·62	trace	trace	trace	0·22	0·18
Potash	2·58	—	0·85	—	0·90	—	1·28	1·89	1·36	2·10	3·42	1·27
Soda	1·82	—	1·20	—	1·06	—	2·27	2·12	1·92	0·92	1·16	2·00
Lead oxide	0·55	6·50	1·75	—	0·36	—	3·73	0·60	1·50	0·67	0·43	—
Total	100·94	96·24	99·76	95·21	99·67	95·55	100·60	100·29	100·84	100·81	98·70	100·65

Reproduced from *Analysed Specimens of English Porcelain* by H. Eccles and H. Rackham, 1922, by courtesy of the Victoria and Albert Museum.

*This analysis was carried out for G. E. Stringer and quoted in his book *New Hall Porcelain*.

again at about 900°C. This sequence of biscuit, higher fired than glaze, was natural to English potters and had been used for the making of Staffordshire earthenware at least since creamware replaced salt-glazed stoneware. On the other hand, Chinese porcelain was made by a different firing sequence. The first firing was at about 900°C, after which the body had completely dried out and lost some water of reaction from the ingredients. However, true fusion had not begun. This body, which was firm enough to handle safely but would not withstand rough usage, was then dipped in glaze before being given its real firing at 1,300–1,400°C. It was during this stage that the body achieved its translucency and, since the glaze matured simultaneously it fused into the underlying body. This sequence of firing was used for making hard-paste porcelain by Cookworthy at Plymouth and by Champion at Bristol, which suggests how the definition embracing both process and materials developed. But it need not always be so and New Hall was the first factory to combine the hard-paste materials by the more English firing sequence of high-temperature biscuit followed by lower-temperature glaze. This achievement was a major breakthrough in porcelain manufacture, though we do not know who made it. Was it Champion's final success or was it the first achievement of the Staffordshire potters? I favour the latter view but there is no evidence. There is evidence, however, that hard-paste porcelain can be made by ·this process, for unglazed pieces of hard-paste biscuit porcelain have been dug up on the site of the Caughley factory in Shropshire.[4]

The principal differences between Bristol and New Hall porcelain lay in the process by which they were made, and in the glaze. The original Bristol glaze had to be modified so that it could be formed at a lower temperature and this was probably done by adding fluxes. Certainly lead was used, for the one hundred New Hall pieces which I have tested all contained a good proportion of lead.[5] I have not, however, found lead in any Bristol glazes that I have tested. In the beginning this new glaze had poor flow properties and often lay thickly on a piece. On the bottom of early teapots you see streaks in the glaze as though some excess glaze has been wiped away by drawing the fingers across. On tea-caddies and round teapots the glaze often failed to flow completely and there are patches of raw paste to be seen near the base. When saucers and bowls were stood upside-down for the glaze to drain and dry, small pools of glaze accumulated around the rim. This is often a good aid to recognition. Many eighteenth-century glazes frothed and bubbled when being formed (carbon dioxide is released when the materials interact) and the New Hall

[4]D. F. Holgate, *E.C.C. Trans.*, vol. 6, part 3, 1967, pp. 268–83.

[5]The recipe for 'A China Glaze' (page 31) is perhaps relevant here.

glaze always shows a mass of gas bubbles in it, especially in the thick areas in the footrim and where handle and spout join the body. These probably account for the relatively low gloss of the glaze since the surface is frequently covered with minute burst bubbles. New Hall imitators can often be spotted by their glazes being too shiny.

The presence of wreathing, or spiral marks, on the sides of teapots, jugs and bowls is often said to be a characteristic of Plymouth and Bristol porcelains. It is found on some New Hall wares and also on pieces made by other factories. I believe that it is a mechanical property of the ingredients and is, therefore, likely to be found on pieces of porcelain made by any factory which used a mixture of china-clay and china-stone.

The benefits which came from the improved manufacturing technique were manifold. The firing sequence was the same as that familiar to these Staffordshire potters and the lower firing temperature was more economical in fuel and kiln furniture. The higher Bristol firing temperature must have been difficult to maintain and control and their kiln losses were notoriously high. It is no wonder that from the outset New Hall made a good, consistent product. Above all they were able to make blue-and-white wares transfer-printed underglaze. It has been said that if only Bristol had been able to make ordinary blue-and-white china readily they could have had a more stable financial background. They could not do so because the body, after the first firing, was not really hard enough to withstand the rigours of transfer-application: the New Hall biscuit was. Furthermore, the lower glaze temperature used by New Hall enabled them to produce a more aesthetically pleasing underglaze blue colour.

Before progressing to the change-over from hard-paste porcelain to bone-china we should return to the word-game and the meaning of hard- and soft-paste porcelain as well as a recently introduced phrase 'hybrid-hard-paste' porcelain. Of course, the problems of nomenclature might not have developed if the original adjectives 'true' and 'artificial' had been retained: the former being applied to porcelain made from raw materials 'from the earth' as Cookworthy referred to them. However, the clock cannot be turned back. Any porcelain which is composed principally of china-stone and china-clay must be called 'hard-paste' but, in order to distinguish those factories like Plymouth and Bristol which used the same process as the Chinese from those like New Hall, Coalport and Chamberlain, which used the earthenware and soft-paste porcelain firing sequence, a sub-set can be named 'hybrid hard-paste' porcelain – a hybrid between the hard-paste composition and the soft-paste process. It must be realised, however, that since the term hard-paste is related to the composition of a piece of porcelain then visual examination cannot be used to identify it with certainty; chemical analysis is necessary. On the other hand the method of manufacture can be distinguished often by examination of the glaze/body interface. I will not accept that anyone can look at a piece of porcelain and be able to say with certainty that it is 'hybrid hard-paste' porcelain unless he has first of all identified the factory of manufacture or been able to place it into a recognisable group of porcelain because of its potting features.

New Hall's hard-paste body was made until after 1811. By then its production was well controlled. The body could be finely potted, and the glaze, which contained fewer gas bubbles than in the early years, fitted closely. It is a pity that the standard of decoration was not improved or even maintained. From the beginning of the nineteenth century other factories were making bone-china, a body which consisted of clay, stone and bone ash. The bone ash not only strengthened the body but gave it a very white translucent appearance, a fine foil for coloured enamel decoration. By comparison, New Hall's grey hard-paste must have looked rather dull, so that eventually they must have been forced to change over to the new bone-china formula. Obviously the change-over was achieved without much difficulty, since the New Hall version was a good quality porcelain with a clean, clear glaze. Unfortunately for the collector, most bone-china has a similar appearance, and unless there is some identity mark or novel shape it is very difficult to distinguish one factory's products from another's. In the first years at New Hall the glaze frequently exhibited black specks. Later on, the quality of the paste and glaze was as high as has ever been achieved.

The date of the change from hard-paste to bone-china can only be surmised, but there are facts from which to work. A New Hall invoice dated 1810 describes the factory as making 'real-china' and a hard-paste jug dated 1811 is known (Colour Plate P). In 1810 Peter Warburton enrolled his patent for the application of gold transfer-prints to porcelain. The lowest known pattern using this process is number 846. Furthermore, pattern number 984 is commonly found on both hard-paste and bone-china bodies, and pattern number 1046 is the highest number known on the hard-paste body alone. It would seem that the bone-china body was introduced first when the pattern book was at about number 1000 and this would possibly be about 1814. The change-over could have occurred in any year after 1811 and most writers suggest 1812. Since on average between thirty-five and forty patterns were introduced each year and about one hundred and forty new patterns were used between the enrolment of Peter Warburton's patent and the introduction of the bone-china body I believe that it was closer to 1814.

So far as I am aware, there is no convincing evidence to show that New Hall made earthenware. Why should they even consider such a thing – they were established only to make porcelain?

CHAPTER 6

The Wares

Much porcelain is commonly described as 'New Hall' but by no means all of it was made at the New Hall China Manufactory. One of the reasons for the confusing similarities of style is that there was no patent protection for the shapes of the wares or decoration during the period when New Hall porcelain was made; and the Staffordshire porcelain industry, which was expanding at the time, made many imitations. A detailed knowledge of the wares is necessary before one can recognise and identify them accurately. The most important aids to recognition are details of shape because even when another factory copied a shape their moulds could not be exactly the same, and handles, spouts and knobs, for example, were not always put in exactly the same place.

The following outline of the New Hall wares has been compiled by careful study of the different potting shapes and the patterns which were applied to them. Some patterns originally used during the hard-paste period were repeated on bone-china. Since some of these bone-china pieces bear a New Hall mark, we can be certain of the origin of the pattern and its associated number. The shapes of hard-paste services decorated with this pattern (accompanied by the appropriate number) can then be assigned to New Hall with confidence. For example, the Museum collections at Stoke-on-Trent have a standard London-shape bone-china teapot bearing both the concentric-rings New Hall mark and the number 425 and decorated with the chinoiserie 'window' pattern. They have also four different shapes of hard-paste teapot with this pattern and number. The shape of the sucrier and the jug associated with each teapot shape has been identified in each case by finding a tea-service containing all three pieces. Similar methods have been used to identify the earlier round teapots and the corrugated-moulded tea-wares, working from the silver-shape teapot in the Victoria and Albert Museum collection which has 'Ralph Clewes New Hall fecit' incised in the base (Plate 17). This teapot is a cornerstone of our knowledge of New Hall tea-wares, especially for those made during the first decade.

It appears that production during the hard-paste period falls roughly into three phases. At first the potters experimented, being prepared to make a wide range of products (testing the market). During this period – say 1781 to about 1787 – a characteristic corrugated moulding was applied to some tea-wares (Colour Plate A), a novel overlapping thumb-rest (commonly referred to as a 'clip' (Colour Plate E)) on the handles was used and small silver-shape teapots (Colour Plate I, centre) were introduced. Many tea-sets included a tea-caddy and a spoon-tray. The blue-and-white wares included leaf-shaped pickle-trays, asparagus-shells and knife-handles. Dessert-services were made. Then came a brief transitional period during which this diversity of ware was reduced and the shapes were modified and simplified, until after 1790 a standard silver-shape tea-set, together with services made in the contemporary fashionable taste, was retailed. Throughout the bone-china period the London-shape (Colour Plates Q and R) was used and it seems probable that only towards the end of its life did the factory add any other shape to the range.

TEAPOTS AND STANDS

To speculate is time-consuming but it is all that can be done when considering the first New Hall products, either made with Champion at Keeling's works or after Champion, Turner and Keeling had left and the remainder moved to Shelton Hall. The first products were probably the group which has 'corrugated' moulding over the surface. I give it this name because unlike the ribbed fluting found on later wares (which I call 'reeded') there is a space in between each rib. On cups and small jugs these ribs and spaces are so close together as to give the impression of corrugation but on the larger hot-water jugs and waste-bowls there is a definite flat section between the ribs. The appearance of the body and glaze of some of these pieces is different from those of the later standard wares and the knobs and shapes of the handles are not always consistent with an obvious New Hall attribution. However, I am convinced that this is a group of early products of the factory and it may help the reader to understand the line of argument if I consider the New Hall round teapots first.

There are four basic shapes of teapot with a circular footrim. The simplest globular pot could be the product of any factory (Colour Plates E and I, right). It has a simple footring (with a glazed base within it) and the lid sits on top of and overlaps the collar. Usually the lids are relatively heavy with a solid onion-shaped knob, the steam vent being through the lid nearby. The majority of them are larger than those of other eighteenth-century factories, but the rarer small ones, often with an open-flower finial (Colour Plate G), are incomparable. The spout is of a rather stubby swan-necked shape which is in proportion only with the small-sized pot. It is the handle which is the hallmark of our factory. A thumb-rest is formed by having two pieces of clay overlap and interlock, a feature that was originally called a 'clip' by Mr Geoffrey Grey. This clip handle is a characteristic feature of plain early wares – coffee-pots, teapots, jugs and cups – although on the smaller pieces the modelling is almost lost. The last recorded pattern number with this handle is 186, which suggests that it was a feature only until about 1787 and that these wares can be dated to the period 1781 to 1787, which was devoted largely to experimentation. I should point out here that although some large jugs of a later date are known with a modification of this handle, I do not consider that this disproves or contradicts the proposed dating. Many of these jugs (e.g. Colour Plate O) were made for presentation.

Barrel-shaped teapots can look ponderous, especially when they have the small swan-necked spout already mentioned (Plate 11). This is possibly why it was changed to have an almost straight upper line with a gentle ogee-curve beneath (Plate 12). The almost flat lid fits inside a circular collar and there is no significant footring, merely a slight glazed recession. We meet for the first time a general, but not invariable, rule differentiating plain from moulded wares.[1] In this case where the teapot is plain (Colour Plate E), the knob is a plain shape and the handle has a clip, but when the body is faceted or reeded the knob is like a pine-cone and the handle is a plain strap (Plate 13 shows a faceted example). The terminals of most handles are semicircular but on the moulded wares they are V- or arrowhead-shaped.

A distinctive feature of the third group (Plate 15) is the definite angular line of the body before it meets the footring. This seems to be a New Hall characteristic. The lid, which on the plain variant has a solid onion-shaped knob and on the moulded pots has a pine-cone knob, sits on top of a shallow rim or collar.[2] The spout, as on most of the barrel-shaped pots, has a straight upper line with an ogee-curved line

[1] In this context plain means that the surface of the clay was smooth with no extra moulding, to distinguish it from the surfaces with additional moulding in the form of reeds, facets or spiral flutes.

[2] A few examples with a ring knob are known, e.g. Plate 100.

6.   TEAPOT illustrated by Ll. Jewitt (op. cit., vol. 2, fig. 460) and said to be painted by Fidelle Duvivier. *See page 54.*

7.   TEAPOT with corrugated moulding and scroll handle and painted in enamels (pattern 3). Height 17.3 cm (6.8 in), hard-paste, 1782–5. *See page 54.*

8.   Barrel-shaped TEAPOT with corrugated moulding and scroll handle and painted in enamels (pattern 78). Height 15.2 cm (6 in), hard-paste, 1782–5. *See page 54.*

9. Part TEA-SET painted in underglaze dark-blue and gold.
The handle, stubby spout and knob are typical of early New
Hall teapots.
Height 16 cm (6.3 in), hard-paste, 1782–7. *Godden Collection.*
See page 54.

10. Part TEA- and COFFEE-SERVICE painted in green enamels and
gold. Early services contained a tea-caddy and a spoon-tray.
Teapot height 17 cm (6.7 in), hard-paste, 1782–7.
See pages 54, 70.

beneath. However, some of these spouts, notably those on reeded and faceted coffee-pots, have a chain of husks encircling them and a peculiarly scratch-marked section of ten facets (Plate 15, left) between the base of the spout and the husks. The handle is a plain broad strap, which on the plain pot has a backward pointing thumb-rest, but is unadorned when the teapot is reeded (Plate 14) or faceted.

Llewellynn Jewitt illustrated a teapot, which I call 'urn-shaped', decorated by Duvivier (Plate 6). This is a most important linking shape since plain specimens are known with both the same handle (Plate 9) and with a clip handle (Plate 10), and corrugated examples are found with the same handle (Colour Plate A). A corrugated version is also found with an overlapping, double scroll handle (Plate 7). The urn-shaped teapot stands on a very small pedestal base and the lid fits almost flush on the sloping shoulders of the teapot. Usually the end of the spout has six shallow grooves and the bottom of it is encircled with a distinctive leaf-moulding, frequently picked out with gold.

The case for a New Hall provenance for the corrugated wares is strengthened by the existence of a barrel-shaped teapot with an overlapping double scroll handle similar to the one mentioned in the previous paragraph (Plate 8).

The subject of round teapots cannot be left without mentioning the unusual. A unique teapot (Colour Plate I, left) could be a missing Bristol-link. The husk-moulded handle, so typical of Champion's Bristol wares, is married to a globular teapot with a flush-fitting lid – rather reminiscent of creamware 'melon' teapots. The fate of Champion's Bristol moulds has never been revealed. Although Bevis Hillier[3] has shown that John Turner made some stoneware figures of the *Seasons* which closely resembled the Champion figures I cannot claim the same for this husk-moulded handle. It is not from the same mould as any Bristol handle that I have so far seen. On the other hand the spout, with its leaf-moulding, and the lower part of the pedestal base of this teapot link well with the urn-shaped teapots. The acorn knob, sitting on a spray of crisply moulded oak leaves, is unknown elsewhere.

The unusual drum-shaped teapot (Plate 16) would seem to have been made when the urn-shaped teapot gave way to the silver-shape one. Two examples are known, one with an ogee-curved faceted spout, and the other with a straight spout with the oak-leaf moulding beneath it which is commonly found on the small silver-shape teapots. Whilst the lid of the first teapot fits flush with the shoulder of the pot, in the other example there is a shallow collar. *En suite* with these teapots were a low cream-jug (cf. Plate 34) and the covered pear-shaped jug also illustrated in Plate 16.

[3]Bevis Hillier, op. cit., p. 37.

11. Barrel-shaped TEAPOT with stubby
     curved spout and clip handle and
     painted in enamels (pattern 22).
     Height 15.2 cm (6 in), hard-paste,
     1782–7. *See page 51.*

13. Barrel-shaped TEAPOT with faceted
     moulding, pine-cone moulded knob
     and plain loop handle and painted in
     enamels (pattern 78).
     Height 14.6 cm (5.75 in), hard-paste,
     1782–7. *See page 51.*

12. Barrel-shaped TEAPOT with straight
     spout and clip handle and painted in
     pink and magenta enamels.
     Height 15.2 cm (6 in), hard-paste,
     1782–7. *See page 51.*

14. TEAPOT with reeded moulding,
     pine-cone moulded knob and plain
     loop handle and painted in enamels
     (pattern 122).
     Height 17.8 cm (7 in), hard-paste,
     1782–7. *See page 54.*

15. Two TEAPOTS of the same general shape but with different spouts and painted in enamels (pattern 121). The moulding on the spout of the left-hand teapot is found also on the spouts of reeded and faceted coffee-pots (Plates 30 and 31).
Height (*left*) 16.5 cm (6.5 in), hard-paste, 1782–7. *Vincent Thomas Antiques.*
See pages 51, 54.

16. Drum-shaped TEAPOT and COVERED JUG decorated in gold.
Teapot height 14.5 cm (5.7 in), hard-paste, 1782–7. *See page 54.*

The morphological development of the silver-shape teapot (Plate 17), always spoken of as being typical of New Hall, can be traced in a most interesting manner. Evidence of the aptness of its name is found in silver teapots of this shape with contemporary hallmarks. These teapots have a straight tapering spout which is also found on the earliest porcelain examples. However, the silversmiths were not the originators of this spout; the Chinese featured it on their porcelain and the Staffordshire potters on their redwares and basaltes. On the other hand these early New Hall teapots did have one unusual feature (Plate 18) in that they rested upon four small rosettes, each with six petals around the central pistil. It has been suggested that these rosettes were to raise the pot from the table to prevent marking it, but they are not really big enough and besides, teapot stands have been found *en suite*.

During the experimental and transitional phases the basic shape of the silver-shape teapot remained static and the lid always fitted within a raised circular collar: it was the spout and handle which changed. The handle, which developed from the plain one on some of the globular pots, is found now with a herring-bone moulding and narrows before both the upper and lower terminals. As noted previously, the arrow-like terminals are quite characteristic of early teapots, though some specimens are found whose handle terminals are beautifully moulded like shells. The straight tapering spout always had oak-leaf moulding on the underside and this was often attractively outlined with magenta or gold (Plate 18). When the spout changed to the more normal S-shape it still had leaf-moulding around the base and six shallow grooves running its full length, features found on the urn-shaped teapot. The final curved spout had facets on each side which were connected at the top and bottom by curved surfaces. There are a large number of different combinations of these features and the possibilities are multiplied by the appearance of reeded and faceted sides as well as various sizes of teapots. The lids, usually convex, went through a stage of being quite flat and, in the case of reeded and faceted specimens, had similar moulding. The knobs, as with those on the globular teapots, were initially solid and then flask-shaped with a central vent-hole: solid pine-cone knobs accompanied the faceted and reeded pots.

With few exceptions, the silver-shape teapots described so far have been of comparatively small size (base 12.7 by 10.8 cm (5 by 4.25 in)), that is, smaller than most of the globular pots, and one of them is unusually small (base 11.4 by 10.2 cm (4.5 by 4 in)). Considering their size, the obvious lines of development and the low numbers of the patterns found on them, we can be confident that they were the products of the first period of New Hall manufacture – the period of experiment and development between 1781 and 1787. At the end of this period came the larger

17. Silver-shape TEAPOT painted in underglaze mazarine-blue and
     gold (pattern 152). The base bears the unique incised
     inscription 'Ralph Clewes New Hall fecit'.
     Height 15.3 cm (6 in), hard-paste, 1787–90. *Victoria and Albert
     Museum. See pages 50, 57.*

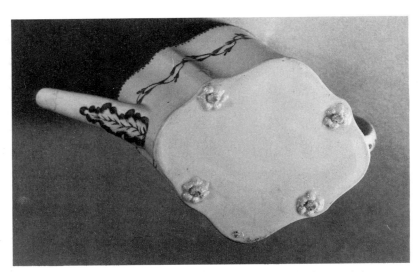

18. TEAPOT BASE showing the four applied rosette feet and the
     leaf-moulding, outlined with magenta enamel, on the
     underside of the spout. *See page 57.*

19. Silver-shape TEAPOT with applied curved fluting decorated in gold (pattern 198).
Height 15.3 cm (6 in), hard-paste, 1787–90. *Godden Collection.*
See pages 59, 132.

transitional teapots which were made before production settled down to the standard plain silver-shape with a smooth ear-shaped handle (pushed in rather than a full loop), no rosette feet, an S-curved spout and flask-shaped knob on the lid with its centrally-bored vent-hole. There were three transitional variants with reeds (Colour Plate J), straight facets, and ogee-curved flutes (Plate 19) between the straight vertical ridges found on all the other teapots. It is important in the case of the latter variant to remember that the straightness of these ridges was retained, for two of the New Hall imitators made teapots on which the line of the ridges followed the curves of the flutes (Plate 121). The lids of these teapots had shallow moulding matching that found on their sides and the knobs were usually solid pine-cones, the steam vent-hole being through the lid. The handles retained the herring-bone moulding of the earlier smaller prototypes but the ends of the handles were not always arrow-shaped. They became rounded and the handle itself lost the pronounced narrowing at each end which was a feature of the earlier ones.

Although some of these transitional styles give a pleasant visual effect this is not always the case: it varied with the decoration and the way in which the lid and the collar sat on the body. No wonder the plain silver-shape became standard. Its general appeal is reflected in the fact that it was made by New Hall until at least 1803 (there is a teapot in the Victoria and Albert Museum inscribed 'Sophia Sayer 1803') and that it was copied at other factories. The commonest patterns found on the transitional shapes are numbered between 150 and 210, which suggests that the transition period was between 1787 and 1789.

The globular teapots were the subject of experiment but never really became established and the silver-shape teapot went through a series of interesting and often attractive modifications before assuming the typical New Hall shape. This makes a neat story of the first eight years or so of the factory's life. On the other hand, it seems likely that a new shape was introduced during these transitional years – the pot with an oval base and a waisted profile on which is superimposed curved fluting (Plate 20). Consideration of the date of this shape offers a timely reminder to the collector to exercise care when using pattern numbers as evidence for the dating of wares. Pattern 52, obviously first used in the opening years of the factory's life, has been recorded on a service featuring this shape. Careful consideration suggests that this is a case of an early pattern being reissued on a later shape, because the glaze under the base of the teapot was well controlled and did not show the thick streaks so often found on the early silver-shape teapots, and the cream-jug was the rather heavy, waisted, obconical shape featured in the transitional period (Plate 40). It would seem then that this shape was introduced at the end of the 1780s and was most popular during the 1790s, since the commonest patterns to appear on it are between the numbers 250 and 350. Plain as well as reeded and faceted variants were made. New Hall was not the only factory to make this shape of teapot and examples are frequently found made by Barr or Chamberlain at Worcester and by John Rose of Coalport when he was using the Caughley works after 1799. The depth of the footring, the profile of the lid and the shape of the knob are identification features of the New Hall teapots and, in the case of the spirally fluted ones, the shallow and gentle character of the fluting.

Much of the excitement of collecting teapots is lost when the factory's production is established, for there are fewer interesting prototypes and modifications. Large oval-based teapots were introduced with either straight vertical sides (Plate 21)[4] or gentle convex curved sides (Plate 22). This latter shape was also made with spiral fluting decorating the body. On the straight vertical-sided teapot the curved spout had an octagonal cross-section and the handle was a plain loop fitted on to the side of the pot in the same way as on the standard silver-shape teapot, including the rounded terminal shape. The handle shape and the manner of attachment often help to distinguish it from teapots of similar shape made by the Caughley-Coalport,

---

[4]This shape is referred to as 'Old Oval Shape' in Spode's Shape Book, 1820.

20. Oval waisted TEAPOT with applied curved fluting and painted in enamels. Enamelled pattern number 328. Height 17.8 cm (7 in), hard-paste, 1790–7. *See page 60.*

21. 'Old oval shape' TEAPOT decorated with a black bat-print and gold. Enamelled pattern number 559. Height 16 cm (6.3 in), hard-paste, 1795–1805. *See page 60.*

22. TEAPOT with oval base and convex-curved sides painted in enamels. Enamelled pattern number 593.
Height 16.5 cm (6.5 in), hard-paste, 1795–1805. *See pages 60, 64.*

Minton, Spode, Miles Mason and Herculaneum factories. The lids fitted almost flush inside the very narrow retaining-rim, and although the lid frequently had the under flange cut away to accommodate a small apron across the front of the opening of the teapot, it was not an invariable feature. The lids had a vent-hole in front of the knob, which was of a solid oval shape with a small pimple on the top. The spout of the convex-sided pot had a smooth oval cross-section and was very much more bulbous where it joined the body than it was at the open end. The oval knob had a ridge like a mould-mark running around it which was often picked out by the decoration. The wide range of patterns found on these two shapes suggests that they were introduced during the 1790s and were still made in the first decade of the nineteenth century.

As the eighteenth century drew to a close New Hall introduced a new shape of teapot which they made until the time came to change over from hard-paste to bone-china. 'Boat-shape' (Plate 23) is the appropriate name given to this bulbous oval teapot, the collar of which rises up and flares out like a ship's prow. In the earlier specimens there is a balanced rhythm in the shape of the teapot which invites one to hold it and pour tea from it. In the later years the teapot grew in size so that

23. TEAPOT of smaller boat-shape painted in enamels. Enamelled pattern number 603.
Height 14 cm (5.5 in), hard-paste, 1795–1805. *City Museum and Art Gallery, Stoke-on-Trent. See pages 62, 64.*

24.   'New oval shape' TEAPOT painted in enamels. Enamelled pattern number 748.
Height 17.8 cm (7 in), hard-paste, 1805–10. *See page 64.*

25.   'New oval shape' TEAPOT with a modified handle form and painted in enamels. Enamelled pattern number 1040.
Height 17.8 cm (7 in), hard-paste, c. 1810. *See page 64.*

although the line remained, the whole effect became rather ponderous. The plain loop handle started directly from the rim of the collar and had a slight but definite kick away from the body, which it joined above the footrim. The narrowing spout was of a pronounced triangular section and often at the end had a knurled or thickened upper edge. The lid, which fitted well inside the collar, had no flange and was dome-like with a solid oval knob similar to that on the oval straight-sided teapot. Some knobs were made to represent the fleur-de-lis (Plate 58). The colouring of the lily was in keeping with the decoration of the teapot.

A problem is posed by the teapot whose handle had a strut between the body and the normal upper connecting end of the handle (Plate 24).[5] It is most likely that it was a modification of the boat-shaped teapot, although it is possible that it was a precursor of it, somewhere between the oval-based convex-sided pot (Plate 22) and the boat-shaped pot (Plate 23).[6] It is not a very elegant style and when the decoration on it is uninspired it can be downright ugly; it is no wonder that not very many were made. The diagnostic features are the symmetrically curved collar inside which fits the rather high-domed lid; the knob, which has a thick stem to attach it to the lid, and is a solid oval with a little pimple on top of it; and the spout, which has a similar cross-section to that of the boat-shaped teapot. The most important feature, however, is the handle, which apart from the small strut already mentioned has a forward pointing thumb-rest, an unusual feature for a New Hall teapot handle. For a short time a handle variant was introduced (Plate 25).

The New Hall China Manufactory commenced with some interesting and attractive shapes and experimented in order to produce a popular range of wares; and yet, when they changed over to the bone-china body, they appear for most of the time to have made only one shape of teapot, which was similar to that produced by almost all the contemporary factories – it was called the 'London-shape' (Colour Plate Q and Plate 27). This teapot had a rectangular base, lid-opening and lid, and its sides were characteristically bulbous with a definite concave section below the top flange in which sat the lid. The handle had a characteristic shape which represented a complete change from those we have seen so far. On the other hand, the spout seems to have developed from that of the boat-shaped teapot. Only one size of teapot was normally made but I have seen a smaller teapot which appeared to have been made from a sucrier body on which a spout had replaced one of the handles.

[5]This shape is referred to as 'New Oval Shape' in Spode's Shape Book, 1820.

[6]Another intermediate shape of teapot is illustrated by P. Miller and M. Berthoud in *An Anthology of British Teapots*, 1985, Plate 1344. I believe that the illustrated example is of hard-paste (not bone-china as described) since the decoration is of c. 1800 and the recorded examples of cream-jugs which have a similar body and handle form were of the hard-paste body.

26. Transitional TEAPOT decorated with a black bat-print and gold. Whilst this is a bone-china teapot, examples of this shape are known made in the hard-paste body. It was obviously made when New Hall was changing over from one body to the other. Pattern number 1147 in gold.
Height 15 cm (5.9 in), bone-china, 1810–15. *See page 66.*

27. London-shape TEAPOT painted in underglaze mazarine-blue and gold. Enamelled pattern number 1059.
Height 15.3 cm (6 in), bone-china, 1815–25. *See page 64.*

28. Wicker-moulded TEAPOT decorated with transfer-prints overpainted with enamels and gold. Enamelled pattern number 2082.
Height 19 cm (7.5 in), bone-china, 1825–30. *Norfolk Museums Service (Norwich Castle Museum). See page 66.*

This London-shape was not an entirely new shape for the New Hall range, since an obvious forerunner was introduced at the end of the hard-paste period (Plate 26). Essentially it was the imposition of a rectangular ground-plan upon the boat-shaped teapot, with a new handle form which did occasionally occur on the earlier 'new oval shape' teapot (Plate 25). It is found in both hard-paste and bone-china and can thus be called a true transitional shape.

Later on, the London-shape teapot was made with a more vigorously shaped handle which made the body appear to be more bulbous (Colour Plate R). It looks very attractive when basket-weave moulding has been applied to the body (Plate 28). A cautionary word should be uttered here, for I believe that other factories used this wickerwork moulding on a London-shape teapot as well as New Hall.

To a large extent the story of the teapot is the story of New Hall. Positive identification of its wares depends so much upon a knowledge of teapot shapes that it is very important to know the standard range. By linking the piece in a service with a teapot of known shape an intelligible outline of the factory's production can often be ascertained by comparison with related standard pieces. The teapot in every service had a stand but, although the simple shape of the stand makes it less susceptible to damage than the teapot, fewer seem to have withstood the passage of time. Quite naturally, they echoed the shape of the base of the teapot and if there is doubt about the provenance of the stand then its proportion and size can be used as evidence. The majority of New Hall teapot stands had a flat unglazed base. In particular, this applied to the stands made for the silver-shape, the straight-sided and the ogee-waisted oval-based teapots. When the silver-shape teapot was reeded, faceted or fluted, this moulding was always followed by the side of the stand. Moulding enhanced their appearance and many of them are very attractive indeed.

The early round teapot stand looked rather like a small plate and could on first acquaintance be taken for one. However, instead of the simple upward curve to the rim which is found on saucers and plates the shape was more sinuous and curved back to form a shallow everted rim. A small footrim is found on the stands which accompany the boat-shaped and oval-based, convex-sided teapots. This must have improved the insulation between the hot teapot and the table and thus reduced the number of heat marks on table tops. Such footrims were usually shallow and formed by hollowing out the centre of the base. By this means the apparent outer edge of the footrim was actually a continuation of the side of the stand. Unlike the other teapot stands they had the enclosed central part glazed. The bone-china teapot stand had a shallow footrim and was glazed underneath.

29.   COVERED HOT-WATER JUG painted in gold (pattern 52) and COFFEE-POT painted in enamels (pattern 20).
Height of both 24.2 cm (9.5 in), hard-paste, both are 1782–7. *See pages 70, 78.*

30.   COFFEE-POT with reeded moulding and moulded pine-cone knob and painted in
      enamels. Enamelled pattern number 195.
      Height 26 cm (10.25 in), hard-paste, 1787–90. *Godden Collection. See page 70.*

31. COFFEE-POT with faceted moulding and moulded pine-cone knob and painted in gold. Note the chain of husks on the spout picked out with gold. Mark: 'No 52' in gold.
Height 23.1 cm (9.1 in), hard-paste, 1787–90. *See page 70.*

COFFEE-POTS AND STANDS

The number of coffee-cups that can be found suggests that they were popular pieces and used widely. This is belied by the small number of coffee-pots that have survived, and the paltry number of different styles created. In fact, all the hard-paste coffee-pots had a similar silhouette (Plates 29–31 and Colour Plate M). The early spouts were more like a swan's neck than the later ones, the typical clip handle preceded a plain loop and the line of the bulbous body became more ponderous as time went on. Reeded, faceted and spiral-fluted coffee-cups were made and so it seems likely that such moulding was used on the coffee-pots although the spiral-fluted variant has not been recorded yet. As was said earlier in connection with teapots, the spout of the reeded and faceted variant is encircled with a chain of husks and the knob is a moulded pine-cone (Plates 30 and 31).

The bone-china coffee-pot is of a completely different shape (Plate 32), clearly belonging to a different era. The illustrated example bears the concentric-rings mark.

The stands for the coffee-pots resemble modern tea-plates. The footrim has all the typical New Hall characteristics and the flange resembles a narrow, gently everted rim.

JUGS

Some of the most attractive and desirable pieces of porcelain made by any factory are cream-jugs and those made at New Hall, especially in the early years, are no exception to this rule. Most can be classified readily and coupled with a related teapot shape, but occasionally an unusual specimen turns up to make the collector's life interesting and ensure that his collection is never complete.

First there are the pear-shaped, corrugated-moulded jugs (Colour Plate A) whose rather elongated spouts have three radiating ribs on the underside. Whilst those decorated with gilding usually have a lid, those with enamel decoration are without. Then there are plain jugs with a clip handle and a small spout with leaf-moulding round the base, perhaps the most commonly found. They also have a lid (Plate 10). Other variations occur with a sparrow-beak (Plate 33) and with a flared pouring spout (Colour Plate G). Whilst decoration in gold, coloured enamels and blue-and-

32. Bone-china COFFEE-POT painted in enamels (pattern 1084). Mark: 'New Hall' within
two concentric rings.
Height 22.2 cm (8.75 in), 1814–30. *Victoria and Albert Museum. See page 70.*

white is known on the sparrow-beak jugs, so far only blue-and-white decoration has
been noted on those with the flared spout.

Two other styles of jug which were made to accompany a globular or a drum-
shaped teapot may conveniently be mentioned here. The small round jug (Plate 127)
with a beak spout is one of the prettiest pieces I have seen. 'Robin jug' springs to
mind as an apt description. It was thrown on the wheel and is found with either a
plain loop or a clip handle. The other jug is of faceted sauceboat-shape (Plate 34).

The first style to be commonly used was helmet-shaped and copied from silver. A
few were corrugated (Plate 35) and, since all of those that I have seen appear to be

33. Sparrow-beak COVERED JUG painted in gold.
     Height 14.6 cm (5.75 in), hard-paste, 1782–7. *Godden Collection. See page 70.*

34. Faceted JUG painted in enamels (pattern 67).
Height 8.3 cm (3.3 in), hard-paste, 1782–7. *See pages 54, 71.*

35. Helmet-shaped JUG with corrugated moulding painted in enamels (pattern 20).
Height 9.9 cm (3.9 in), hard-paste, 1782–5. *See page 71.*

36. Three helmet-shaped JUGS in graduated sizes painted in enamels (*left*: pattern 139; *centre*: pattern 98).
Height (*left*) 11.2 cm (4.4 in); (*centre*) 9.1 cm (3.6 in); (*right*) 8.1 cm (3.2 in). Hard-paste, 1782–90. *See page 74.*

made of a recognisable grey body and glaze, the New Hall attribution for corrugated wares is supported. The majority of helmet-shaped jugs were made to go with globular, early and transitional silver-shape teapots. Three sizes were made (Plate 36) and these were found reeded (Plate 151) and faceted (Plate 157) as well as plain. The largest jugs usually went with the large silver-shape teapot made during the transitional period. The plain jugs feature the clip handle which was noted on the globular teapot, and on the large plain jug there is an outward kink above the lower terminal (Plate 128). A forward or upward pointing thumb-rest has been seen on a few of these jugs instead of the customary clip handle but apparently this was not a standard feature. However, reeding (Plate 151) and faceting (Plate 157) on the body was considered to be sufficient embellishment, so that invariably the handle became a plain loop.

The bodies of most of these jugs were almost round but some had pushed-in sides which then appear almost triangular. There was a clip handle on the smaller size (Plate 150) and a plain loop on the larger size (Plate 37).

It was quite a natural development from these to the various forms of what has been called the obconical jug. These varied in size and, as with the helmet-shaped jug, were plain (Plate 39), reeded (Plate 143) and faceted (Plate 207). In some cases, when a suitable decoration was applied, these jugs looked very neat and attractive but on other examples, for instance the waisted variant with curved fluting (Plate 40), the effect could be ponderous. It is possible that the attempt to apply spiral fluting to the helmet-shaped jug led to the creation of the obconical jug, which was introduced during the transitional period 1787–90: the jug shown in Plate 153 could well have been one such attempt. These jugs accompanied both silver-shape and oval-based waisted teapots and were in production until almost the end of the century.

We are now at the stage when the jug bore a likeness to the teapot it accompanied (Plate 38). The smaller silver-shape jug (height 9 cm (3.6 in)) is quite charming and generally seems to be decorated in a much neater manner than the run-of-the-mill larger one (height 10.8 cm (4.3 in)). I have not seen a faceted variant but there was a reeded one and there were two versions with curved fluting: on one of these the flutes went round the jug continuously (Plate 235) and on the other the vertical ridges of the plain jug were retained in the manner of the matching teapot (Plate 165). These jugs were originally designed to accompany the silver-shape teapot but they were also included in services with the oval-based, waisted teapot.

An oval straight-sided jug (Plate 41) went with the oval straight-sided teapot and the sides had gentle convex curves when the teapot had convex sides (Plate 42). This latter teapot and jug are also known with spiral fluting (Plate 245). These jugs had a shallow recess under the base which usually showed the characteristic New Hall

37. JUG painted in apricot-peach enamel and gold (pattern 167). This is the larger size of this shape of jug and it has a plain loop handle. The smaller size of jug (Plate 150) has a clip handle.
Height 10.2 cm (4.0 in), hard-paste, 1787–93. *City Museum and Art Gallery, Stoke-on-Trent. See page 74.*

38.   Silver-shape JUG painted in enamels. Enamelled pattern
      number 449.
      Height 10.7 cm (4.2 in), hard-paste, 1790–1805. *See page 74.*

39.   Obconical-shaped JUG painted in
      enamels. Enamelled pattern
      number 338.
      Height 11.4 cm (4.5 in), hard-paste,
      1790–7. *See page 74.*

40.   Obconical-shaped JUG with curved
      fluting and painted in underglaze
      mazarine-blue and gold. Enamelled
      pattern number 243.
      Height 12.2 cm (4.8 in), hard-paste,
      1790–7. *See pages 60, 74.*

41.   JUG which accompanies the 'new oval shape' teapot painted in enamels. Enamelled pattern number 605.
Height 11.4 cm (4.5 in), hard-paste, 1795–1805. *See page 74.*

42.   JUG painted in underglaze mazarine-blue, enamels and gold. Pattern number 484 in gold.
Height 11.4 cm (4.5 in), hard-paste, 1795–1805. *See page 74.*

bubbled glaze. The plain loop handle came from the back of the rim and rejoined the body about one inch above the base; and the concave neck-band continued even under the handle, which usually distinguishes this New Hall jug from those made by the other factories using a similar style.

There were two jugs to match the boat-shaped teapot. Predictably, the first one was the more elegant (Plate 43), matching the low, boat-shaped pot. The later, larger and more bulbous version (Plates 250 and 302) was in keeping with the ornate gilt decoration which was usually applied to it: it was first made at the turn of the century. The handle on these jugs was a plain loop with a slight kick away from the body at its lower junction with it, but occasionally a forward-pointing thumb-rest on the top of the loop is found (Plate 283). The latter jug probably accompanied the teapots shown in Plates 24 and 25, since in both cases the handle has this feature.

When the rectangular-plan teapot was introduced shortly before the change-over from the hard-paste to the bone-china body, it had a matching jug (Plate 44) which was not a very elegant shape. It is a relief to find that the line was changed drastically when the standard bone-china shape was introduced. The jug was longer, with a smooth rim- and spout-line, and a clean handle shape with a small internal projecting cusp about one inch above the lower junction with the body. This shape was used with tea-services throughout the bone-china period (Plate 45). Naturally when the more vigorously shaped handle was introduced to the teapot it appeared also on the jug (Plate 46); and similarly when basket-weave moulding was applied to the tea-wares towards the end of the bone-china period.

Large jugs were made throughout the life of the factory, but they were never common or standard wares. The first ones may have been hot-water jugs since some of them have a cover (Plate 29, left). They are adaptations of the coffee-pot with the long spout replaced by a large beak-like spout. Both corrugated and plain examples are known. Sometimes on the unmoulded clip-handled jugs there are three moulded ribs on the underside of the spout rising from a raised point where it meets the body – a feature more commonly found on the corrugated jugs.

The most distinctive group of hard-paste jugs had a modification of the early clip handle; the lower section had an overlapping scroll by which device it changed its shape from a concave to a convex curve, ending in a free outward-pointing cusp (it should be noted particularly that the lower section overlaps outside the end of the upper section). Most of these jugs were made for presentation, for they are extremely well decorated and often have added initials (Colour Plate O). A few were decorated with a standard pattern and were marked with the relevant pattern number, e.g. 241 and 425. These jugs were probably made from 1790 onwards (see page 126).

43. Boat-shaped JUG painted in enamels. Enamelled pattern number 353. Height 7 cm (2.8 in), hard-paste, 1795–1805. *See page 78.*

45. London-shape JUG painted in enamels. Enamelled pattern number 1403. Height 8.4 cm (3.3 in), bone-china, 1815–25. *See page 78.*

44. Bone-china JUG decorated with a bat-print in black named 'View from Eltham'. Pattern number 709 in black. This shape of jug was also made in hard-paste.
Height 8.4 cm (3.3 in), 1810–5. *See page 78.*

46. London-shape JUG with a more angular handle decorated in underglaze pale-blue, enamels and gold. Enamelled pattern number 1696. Height 8.6 cm (3.4 in), bone-china, 1820–30. *See page 78.*

47. WATER-JUG decorated with a bat-print coloured with enamels and gold.
Height 14 cm (5.5 in), bone-china, 1815–25. *City Museum and Art Gallery,
Stoke-on-Trent. See page 80.*

The style of the larger jugs changed as the nineteenth century progressed and the
shape used with the bone-china paste seems to be typical of the period (Plate 47). An
important hard-paste jug must be mentioned here (Colour Plate P), bearing the
inscription 'John Brown, Yoxall, 1811'; it provides good evidence that in this year
New Hall was still using the hard-paste body.

I cannot leave the topic of hard-paste jugs without mentioning three smaller but
very interesting examples. Since all of them were made from moulds there must
surely be more than the few known examples in existence. Footed jugs are much
more common in silver than in ceramics. Redware and salt-glaze examples were
made by earlier Staffordshire potters but very few were made in porcelain. New
Hall made both a plain one (Plate 106) and one with corrugated moulding (Plate
134). Critical examination suggests that porcelain is really too heavy a medium for
this shape. The third jug (Plate 1) is a most attractive shape and although rare in
New Hall is not uncommon when made by either the Caughley or the Worcester
factories.

48. WATER-JUG decorated in bas-relief with added enamel decoration. Mark: 'New Hall' within two concentric rings.
Height 9.1 cm (3.6 in), bone-china, 1820–30. *City Museum and Art Gallery, Stoke-on-Trent. See page 81.*

49. WATER-JUG decorated in white bas-relief on a lavender-blue ground. Height 11.9 cm (4.7 in), bone-china, 1820–30. *City Museum and Art Gallery, Stoke-on-Trent. See page 81.*

Bas-relief is not commonly applied to bone-china; it is more suitable on stoneware, in which medium John Turner, Adams, Davenport and Wedgwood specialised. Nevertheless, New Hall made bone-china jugs decorated with a bas-relief of a hunting scene or of classical figures (Plate 49) which were given a painted ground of lavender or sometimes orange-pink. The underside of the spout and the handle were moulded in a characteristic way. These jugs must have been popular and several of them have been noted with a name and a date added in gold over the glaze. The dates are usually between 1815 and 1825. Other jugs were made (Plate 48) decorated with a moulded hunting scene but they are not, in my opinion, a credit to the New Hall China Manufactory.

SUGAR-POTS

Sugar-pots are amongst the most charming and distinctive pieces in the eighteenth-century tea-set. The occurrence of them in New Hall services, however, poses some interesting questions which are perhaps more in the field of the economist or sociologist than of the ceramist. Some tea-sets contained a covered sugar-pot, others an open sugar-basin. The tea-sets made during the experimental and transitional periods included covered pots, usually when the decoration was gilt, but the standard services with the silver-shape teapot had an open basin, and these sets were most frequently decorated with polychrome sprig patterns. Furthermore, in the late hard-paste and the bone-china periods, nearly all tea-services had a covered sugar-pot and once more the decoration was mostly an ornately gilt pattern.

Why, in some services, were sugar-pots covered and in others left open? Was it simply because a silver-shape sucrier had no aesthetic appeal or did the social habit of using sugar change? Can significance be attached to the appearance of the covered sugar-pot with gilded patterns and the open basin with a floral sprig pattern? It is probable that gilded wares were for 'Sunday best'. I offer no solution, but the question is intriguing.

The covered sucriers of the early services were simple, round and without handles (Plate 50). They had the same shape of knob on the domed lid as was used on the teapot. These were onion- or flask-shaped on plain sucriers and pine-cone-shaped on the sugar-pots which were reeded (Plate 51), faceted (Plate 132) or covered with curved flutes (Plate 153). These sucriers were made for services which included round teapots and both the small-sized and the larger transitional period silver-shape teapots. Usually they were of a standard, relatively large size but some of those with corrugated moulding, some with flower knobs on the lids (Colour Plate G) and most of those decorated by Duvivier are significantly smaller. Occasionally the round sucriers had a stand, like a small teapot or coffee-pot stand. The diameter was usually 14 cm (5.5 in).

At the end of the period of experimentation, about 1787, some sucriers of the Chinese covered rice-bowl type were made. The one illustrated (Plate 52) is of a rare form and the more commonly found examples, which can be plain (Plate 53), reeded, faceted or spiral-fluted, look like the normal open sugar-basin with the characteristic lid sitting inside a slightly everted rim.

A feature of the next group of covered sugar-pots was the mock ring handles placed at each end. As was pointed out by Dr T. A. Sprague[7] these rings were never completely attached to the body; the rings were made separately and then attached to the body at the top and bottom. It is an important diagnostic point, since almost all other factories included the rings as a part of the body moulding.

Three styles of oval-based sucriers are known. The waisted type matched the teapot in many of its features, the comparatively deep footrim with the deep groove

[7]T. A. Sprague, *Apollo*, October 1950, p. 109.

50. Round SUCRIER painted in underglaze mazarine-blue and gold (pattern 170). Height 14.6 cm (5.75 in), hard-paste, 1782–93. *See page 82.*

52. SUCRIER of rare rice-bowl form painted in gold. Gold pattern number 52.
Height 12.7 cm (5 in), hard-paste, 1785–90. *See page 82.*

51. Round SUCRIER with reeded moulding painted in underglaze mazarine-blue and gold (pattern 154).
Height 12.7 cm (5 in), hard-paste, 1782–90. *See page 82.*

53. Round SUCRIER painted in enamels and gold (pattern 53).
Height 14 cm (5.5 in), hard-paste, 1785–90. *See page 82.*

54. Oval waisted SUCRIER with applied curved fluting painted in underglaze mazarine-
blue and gold. Enamelled pattern number 248.
Height 15.2 cm (6 in), hard-paste, 1790–7. *See page 85.*

55. Oval straight-sided SUCRIER which
accompanies the 'old oval shape'
teapot painted in underglaze
mazarine-blue and gold. Enamelled
pattern number 550.
Height 14 cm (5.5 in), hard-paste,
1795–1805. *See page 85.*

56. Oval SUCRIER with convex-curved
sides painted in enamels and gold
(pattern 426).
Height 13.3 cm (5.25 in), hard-paste,
1795–1805. *See page 85.*

A. Part TEA-SET with corrugated moulding decorated in sepia enamel and gold. Note that the handle shapes are different. The handles on the cups in this service were different again, being of the form shown in Plate 67.
Teapot height 15.9 cm (6.25 in), hard-paste, 1782–5.
Godden Collection. See pages 50, 54, 70, 94.

B. MUG with corrugated moulding decorated in enamels.
Height 8.9 cm (3.5 in), hard–paste, 1782–5. *Godden Collection. See page 96.*

C. Bell-shaped MUG decorated in enamels with the monogram 'AW' in gold. Height 8.9 cm (3.5 in), hard-paste, 1782–5. *Godden Collection. See page 96.*

D. FLASK decorated in enamels with a well-painted flower spray within a pink pseudo-scale border.
Diameter of body 9.5 cm (3.75 in), hard-paste, 1782–5. *See page 101.*

E. TEAPOT with a clip handle, painted in enamels with figures in a horse-drawn trap in a landscape featuring a windmill by Fidelle Duvivier.
Height 16.5 cm (6.5 in), hard-paste, 1782–7. *Godden Collection. See pages 50, 51, 125.*

F. TEA-CADDY and PLATE painted in enamels by Fidelle Duvivier. The plate features a hoopoe bird in a river scene. The mark 'No 5' underneath in brown possibly refers to the blue and gold border.
Diameter 20 cm (7.9 in), height of caddy 10.2 cm (4 in), hard-paste, 1782–7.
See pages 94, 125.

G. TEAPOT, COVERED SUCRIER and JUG decorated with underglaze blue transfer-prints. The flower knobs are rare and the teapot and sucrier are of an unusually small size. The flared spout on the jug is uncommon.
Teapot height 13 cm (5.1 in), sucrier height 10.5 cm (4.1 in), jug height 12 cm (4.7 in), hard-paste, 1782–7. *National Museum of Wales. See pages 51, 70, 82, 116.*

H. CUP and SAUCER, possibly for caudle, decorated with the 'arms of Trotman of Cambridgeshire and Gloucestershire with those of Wardell of Norfolk in pretence' in enamels within a gold border. The cup has a scroll handle and is of the form shown in Plate 125.

Cup height 6 cm (2.4 in), saucer diameter 14.7 cm (5.8 in), hard-paste, c. 1787.

See page 100.

I. Three TEAPOTS decorated in enamels (pattern 20). The one on
    the left has a handle form similar to one used at Bristol. The
    teapot in the middle is an early silver-shape example having a
    straight spout and standing on four rosette feet.
    Teapot (right) height 15.9 cm (6.25 in), hard-paste, 1782–7.
    See pages 50, 51, 54.

J. TEAPOT of silver-shape with reeded moulding, decorated in
    underglaze mazarine-blue and gold (pattern 153).
    Height 16.5 cm (6.5 in), hard-paste, 1787–90.
    See pages 59, 109.

close to where it joins the body, the shape of the flanged lid which slightly overlaps the edge of the body, and the knob on it. Reeded (Colour Plate L), faceted and spiral-fluted (Plate 54) variants are known. Both the straight-sided sucrier (Colour Plate N and Plate 55) and the one with convex sides (Plate 56) matched the shape of the teapot in the set. The lid fitted on a narrow recessed rim and the knob was *en suite*. In the case of the convex-sided sucrier examples with spiral-fluted moulding are known (Plate 226).

Sucriers of two shapes went with the boat-shaped teapots. Both have an oval base with a moderately shallow footrim, and the rather high-domed lid fits inside the collar-band, resting on a small rim. The difference between the two styles is that one has two small plain ear-like loop handles, shorter and less generous than those of other factories (Plate 57), whereas the neck-band on the other sugar-pots rises up to a boat-like prow at both ends and these serve as handles (Plate 225). Modifications of these shapes include inward-pointing thumb-rests on the ear handles and, in the case of the double boat-shaped sucrier, a fleur-de-lis knob (Plate 58), obviously going with the smaller boat-shaped teapot with the same knob.

The shape of the last covered sugar-pots in the New Hall range is predictable: a rectangular base, bulbous body and a rectangular domed lid, fitting inside an undulating collar on the hard-paste original, but resting on a shallow rim set in the flat horizontal shoulder on the standard bone-paste sucrier (Plate 59). The handles in both cases have a shape similar to that used for the teapots. However, bone-china sucriers with small bracket handles (Plate 60) have been recently recognised. They accompanied the teapots with the more vigorously shaped handle and those with the applied basket-weave moulding.

TEA-BOWLS, TEACUPS, SAUCERS, SLOP-BOWLS, PLATES, COFFEE-CUPS, COFFEE-CANS

The identification of a single small piece of a service, like a tea-bowl or saucer, is usually difficult unless you have good experience of the characteristics of the paste and glaze of many different factories. There are few distinctive features of the simple New Hall wares, nor is it possible to present a coherent story of developing style.

Tea-bowls varied widely in size but a common feature of the first period was an everted rim which can be easily detected by touch. The footrim was usually vertical sided with a rounding of the edges of the bottom rim. The most distinctive feature seems to be the glaze, which generally contains numerous gas bubbles, very

57.   Oval SUCRIER with two loop handles painted in underglaze
      mazarine-blue and gold. Enamelled pattern number 924.
      Height 13.3 cm (5.25 in), hard-paste, 1795–1810. *See page 85.*

58.   Oval SUCRIER with fleur-de-lis knob painted in underglaze
      mazarine-blue, enamels and gold. Enamelled pattern number
      446.
      Height 11.4 cm (4.5 in), hard-paste, 1795–1805.
      See pages 64, 85.

59. London-shape SUCRIER painted in underglaze mazarine-blue,
enamels and gold. Enamelled pattern number 1313.
Height 12.7 cm (5 in), bone-china, 1815–25. *See page 85.*

60. SUCRIER with two bracket handles painted in underglaze
mazarine-blue, enamels and gold.
Height 12.7 cm (5 in), bone-china, 1823–8. *Godden Collection.*
See page 85.

61.   TEACUP of Bute-shape decorated in coral enamel and gold (pattern 275). Height 5.7 cm (2.25 in), hard-paste, 1795–1805. *See page 89.*

63.   TEACUP of Bute-shape with oval ring handle decorated with bat-print overpainted in enamels and underglaze mazarine-blue and gold (pattern 1277). Height 5.7 cm (2.25 in), bone-china, 1812–20. *See pages 89, 118.*

62.   TEACUP of Bute-shape with ring handle decorated in underglaze mazarine-blue and gold (pattern 556). Height 5.7 cm (2.25 in), hard-paste, 1800–12. *See page 89.*

64.   TEACUP of London-shape decorated in purple enamel and an orange-yellow rim (pattern 1623). Height 5.7 cm (2.25 in), bone-china, 1818–30. A smaller, demi-tasse size was also made (Plate 351). *See page 89.*

65. TEACUP with oval ring handle
     decorated in enamels (pattern 1915).
     Height 5.7 cm (2.25 in), bone-china,
     c. 1825. *See page 89.*

66. TEACUP with basket-weave moulding
     painted with alternate panels of green
     and blue and enamelled sprays of
     flowers (pattern 2050).
     Height 5.7 cm (2.25 in), bone-china,
     1825–30. *See page 90.*

noticeable wherever the glaze gathers in pools. These are found in curtain-like sections round the rim of the bowl (suggesting that the wares were placed rim downward to drain after being dipped in glaze) and on the inside junction of the footrim and base. On the other hand all traces of glaze were carefully cleaned from the bottom edge of the footrim, that is, the part on which it normally stands. It is very rare indeed to find any trace of glaze on this particular part of hard-paste New Hall wares and one should always suspect as belonging to another factory a piece with a glazed footring. Tea-bowls were made and sold by New Hall until almost the end of the hard-paste period although cups with plain loop handles (Plate 61) were probably introduced about 1795 as an alternative: they had a very shallow, glazed recessed base and are popularly known as Bute-shaped. A few examples of the first teacups have handles which closely resemble the kinked Spode shape (Plate 148). This is the only modification I know of the plain loop. Shallow single or double kinks in handles are the products of other factories. Before the end of the hard-paste period an inner finger-ring was added to the handle (Plate 62) and this style was then continued in the bone-china period, during which time the ring was compressed and became an oval (Plates 63 and 65). The most common shape of bone-china cup has a classical 'Grecian handle' so typical of the 1820 period and used by most contemporary factories (Plate 64). When the wicker-moulding was introduced the handle shape was modified (Plate 66). Since it seems likely that more late bone-china tea-sets will be identified there will be more cup shapes to be recorded. The cups shown in Plates 89, 91 and 93 are likely to be New Hall. Occasionally large breakfast cups are seen. These occur in both hard-paste and bone-china but otherwise have the same outline shape and handle as the teacups.

Since reeded, faceted and curved-fluted ornament was applied to teapots, jugs and sugar-pots during the first and transitional periods the tea-bowls, saucers, coffee-cups, plates and slop-bowls were also made in these styles. The noteworthy points here are that the tea-bowls and coffee-cups had twenty-eight reeds, sixteen facets or twenty curved flutes; the saucers had the same number of reeds and facets but in the case of the curved flutes there were twenty-four. The rarely found reeded cup and saucer which is slightly waisted had only twenty-seven reeds.[8] Other points worth making in connection with the curved fluting are that it always appears to have been spaciously conceived and never looked tight or cramped as was the case with the wares of other factories, and the spines or ribs which separated the flutes were not sharply raised. Since the moulding was shallow, the rims of the cups and bowls showed little sign of it. This is not really surprising, since drinking from a bowl or cup with a pronounced moulding on it would be uncomfortable.

The handles on the corrugated cups are quite distinct. The way in which the lower end joins the body, the two parts overlap and the thumb-rest points upwards, is at variance with these features on most of the similarly moulded pear-shaped jugs. Yet the handle form is consistent on the cups, even as their shape changes from a shallow open cup to a taller narrow one (Plate 67). The importance of finding a complete service can be demonstrated here because without such evidence no one would dare to suggest that in one service the shape of the handles of the teapot, the jug and the cups would be different. Since many of these cups with corrugated moulding have shallow proportions I wonder whether they were not originally introduced as handled teacups as an alternative to the open tea-bowls.

The first obvious coffee-cups had the clip handle (Plate 68) and although there were a few attempts to imitate them these can usually be recognised as imitations, either by the colour and appearance of the body or the inclusion of a small tail on the inside of the loop. The shape and size of these cups varied widely so that it is impossible to classify them, but careful examination of the glaze will always confirm their origin. For a short time, before a plain loop handle was introduced, coffee-cups had a grooved handle similar to that used by many contemporary factories.

[8]The difference in the number of curved flutes on bowls and saucers was first pointed out by Dr Sprague in *Apollo*, August 1950, p. 52.

67. COFFEE-CUP with corrugated moulding painted in enamels (pattern 67).
Height 6.3 cm (2.5 in), hard-paste, 1782–5. *See Colour Plate A and page 90.*

69. COFFEE-CUP with plain loop handle painted in black enamel (pattern 308). Height 6.3 cm (2.5 in), hard-paste. 1790–1800. *See page 92.*

68. COFFEE-CUP with clip handle painted in enamels and gold.
Height 6.3 cm (2.5 in), hard-paste, 1782–7. *See page 90.*

70. COFFEE-CAN with plain loop handle painted in underglaze mazarine-blue and gold (pattern 540).
Height 5.6 cm (2.25 in), hard-paste, 1795–1805. *See page 92.*

71. COFFEE-CAN with ring handle painted in orange enamel and gold (pattern 546).
Height 5.6 cm (2.25 in), hard-paste, 1800–12. *See page 92.*

72. COFFEE-CAN with oval ring handle decorated with a bat-print overpainted with enamels and gold (pattern 984).
Height 5.6 cm (2.25 in), bone-china, 1812–20. *See page 92.*

In the second half of the 1780s plain loop handles were introduced and the shape of the cups became more consistent (Plate 69); as with the tea-bowls, the everted rim was often in evidence. Reeded, faceted and curved-fluted variants were made although, as on the more important pieces, the handles were plain. In fact they were usually strap-like and frequently had pointed terminals similar to those found on some of the early teapots and jugs. The manner in which a handle is attached to the body of a cup is worthy of careful study as also is the shape of the terminal.

About the same time as teacups appeared, New Hall changed from coffee-cups to coffee-cans. They usually had a very slight convex curve to their sides and a plain loop handle (Plate 70), but when finger-rings were introduced to teacup handles, so they were to coffee-cans (Plates 71–2). During the bone-china period the coffee-cups were similar in shape and style of handle to the teacups: they were smaller and very dainty (Plate 351).

The diameter and depth of the saucers varied considerably and generalisation is difficult. However, in the hard-paste period the footrim matched that of the tea-bowl in cross-section, lack of glaze on the actual ring and accumulation of bubbled glaze within the footrim. Often there were curtains of glaze round the outside edge. Moulded saucers are very attractive and are keenly sought after. In general, the sharpness and depth of fluting and reeding is markedly less on New Hall wares than on those of other factories. It is specially the case with the faceted and fluted saucers where the moulding soon merges into a smooth surface. Painting decoration on these saucers must have been much easier than on the partnering cups and bowls. At no time during New Hall's life was a well for the cup made in the bottom of the saucer. Originally this was probably because tea was poured from the tea-bowl into the saucer before it was drunk. The centre of the saucer inside was flat and the sharpness of the upward curve to the rim depended on the depth of the saucer. During the bone-paste period, however, the saucers became deeper and had straight, angled sides from the centre flat area. This shape matched that of the cups admirably.

Slop-bowls were of a remarkably consistent shape and size throughout the hard-paste period. The footrims were quite deep, especially in the first decade, but they were generally larger versions of the tea-bowl footrim, a parallel-sided, rounded footrim with a glaze-free footring and pools of bubbled glaze in the footrim junction with the base. The number of reeds, facets and curved flutes was the same as was used on the tea-bowl. However, there were two profiles in the bone-paste period. One was similar to the hard-paste bowl but with a rounded footrim, and the other had angular sides which matched the outline of the cups.

Bread-plates, throughout the factory's life, were generally without a flange, although a few in early services are like the round teapot-stands with a shallow everted rim. Most plates, like the saucers, were flat with upward curved rims; in fact, they are usually called saucer-dishes. In the early years the plates were shallow and the upward curve was gentle, but as time went by the curve became more pronounced at the edge although the overall depth did not increase very much. Early plates often showed signs of sagging within the footrim, an observation which calls to mind the difficulty which Champion had at Bristol when making flat ware and how he sometimes used an extra support as a remedy.

The occurrence of a few flanged plates creates a problem. In bone-china they were made for dessert-services (e.g. Plate 224) but the use of the hard-paste plates (usually smaller in size than the normal saucer-dish) is obscure.

MISCELLANEOUS WARE

Tea- and coffee-services were the staple productions of the New Hall China Manufactory and all representative collections of the factory's ware are built around their developing shapes. It follows that the collector finds pieces interesting, and in many cases rare, wherever the makers digressed from their main purpose. The kind of piece made of hard-paste porcelain is so different from that made of bone-china that it is more convenient to consider the two groups separately.

Many of the rare and unusual hard-paste pieces were made during the first decade. This was when the manufacturers seem to have been most ambitious and when experiment abounded.

Tea-services were completed with a tea-caddy and a spoon-tray, just as they were when made at Worcester, Caughley and Lowestoft. At New Hall most of these full services were decorated with gilt patterns and only a few bore the simple polychrome sprigs or underglaze blue transfers. The style of decoration found on these services must have been dictated by the public. In the last two decades of the eighteenth century it is probable that blue-and-white decoration and coloured enamels were used on everyday wares but gilt decoration was demanded for 'Sunday best' services.

Even in 1780 tea was a special drink and expensive. The lady of the house took great care of it and often kept it under lock and key. Certainly servants were not always trusted with its care. Thus it was natural for a best porcelain tea-set to have its own caddy. Quite a number have survived but relatively few of these still have a lid. Only one shape of tea-caddy was made with corrugated moulding (Colour Plate A). In fact it is the only one which New Hall made which stood on a domed pedestal base. Plain caddies were mostly of a jar shape with a domed lid overlapping the collar; only a few were made without a collar, the lid fitting flush with the top of the caddy.[9] So many variations occur in the shape of the shoulders and sides that it seems likely that they were hand-thrown (Colour Plate F and Plate 116). The plain knob is so small that it slips easily from the grasp; it is little wonder that few have survived. Surely the highest mortality rate in porcelain affects the tea-caddy lid.

Reeded and faceted tea-sets were made and so we find tea-caddies *en suite*. By contrast with most plain ones, these had no deep collar and their lid, which usually had a small pine-cone knob, fitted flush into the shoulder, held in place by a shallow raised rim (Colour Plate L and Plate 73). These cone knobs were even harder to grasp than the plain ones and they were sometimes replaced by an unmoulded knob deceivingly flecked with gold (Colour Plate L).

The last shape of caddy (Plate 74) matched the silver-shape teapot, but few are seen. The probable reason for this is that the introduction of the silver-shape heralded the end of the factory's experimental period and the beginning of the marketing of standard sets in which fancy extras were no longer included.

[9]One such tea-caddy, decorated with an underglaze blue transfer-print, was exhibited (Cat. No. 64) in the 'New Hall Bicentenary Exhibition 1781–1981' held in the City of Stoke-on-Trent Museum.

73. TEA-CADDY with reeded moulding and moulded pine-cone knob painted in enamels (pattern 139).
Height 11.4 cm (4.5 in), hard-paste, 1785–90. *See page 94.*

74. TEA-CADDY matching a silver-shape teapot painted in enamels (pattern 253).
Height 12.1 cm (4.75 in), hard-paste, 1790–5. *See page 94.*

Spoon-trays are extremely rare, either because fewer were made than even tea-caddies or, more likely, because they were useful as pin-trays when the tea-service was cast aside. The suggestion that they could be used for pins lays emphasis on their size. They were small (14.6 cm (5.8 in) long) and were originally made for holding teaspoons so that the saucer was free to be used for tea-drinking or, perhaps, because teaspoons were too long and heavy to be easily balanced in a saucer. Small teapot stands should not be confused with spoon-trays. A dessertspoon or small tablespoon would be more suitable than a teaspoon for these! Two shapes of spoon-tray are known. One is of quatrefoil form (Plate 152) and the other, like the product of other factories, of long hexagonal shape (Colour Plate L).

According to Jewitt,[10] both dinner- and dessert-services were made, but they are

[10] Ll. Jewitt, op. cit., vol. 2, p. 309.

seldom found. The dessert-services identified so far featured fine moulding which formed the outline of shells. In some cases this moulding was filled with bright-blue lines and the outline completed with gold (Plate 76). Alternatively, a very dark-blue colour formed a border around the edge of the plate up to and around the moulded shells, which were then edged with gold (Plate 75). These must have made handsome but simple services built round lobed plates, some with pierced edges, heart-shaped dishes, tureens and stands; some of the ladles were pierced (Plate 4).

Occasionally a flanged plate is found decorated with a stock pattern (Plate 271) and this possibly belonged to a dessert-service or was ordered specially by a customer as an alternative to a saucer-dish form of bread-plate. In the same way castors (Plate 3) were possibly a special order.

Accessories for the dinner-table such as leaf-shaped pickle-trays (Plate 99) and asparagus-servers (Plate 107) occur only in blue-and-white. Similarly, knife-handles (Plate 101) seem only to bear this type of decoration.

Mugs were made mostly during the first twenty years of the factory's life. Well-potted barrel-shaped specimens appear in the corrugated period (Colour Plate B), followed by bell-shaped mugs (Colour Plate C) and very fine crisp leaf-moulded examples in different sizes (Plate 77). Plain cylindrical mugs whose loop handle had a backward-pointing thumb-rest were made later (Plate 160). Some of the quart size had a slightly tapering neck-band – a feature found on some contemporary stoneware mugs (Plate 223). Bone-china mugs were made with bas-relief moulded classical designs on a lavender-blue ground (Plate 94) and coloured hunting scenes (Plate 95, right).

Moulded wares occur as a minor part of the New Hall range. Like many other factories New Hall made two sizes of cream-jugs which feature moulded leaves rising up from the base (Plates 79 and 80). The contemporary names are low- and high-Chelsea ewer. The smaller size seems to be the more elegant, but both are attractive and can be found decorated with early standard polychrome patterns as well as underglaze blue transfer-prints. Their handles form their most important feature, with the thumb-rest piece at the top and the overlapping piece in the middle. Usually there is leaf-moulding below the thumb-rest and, on the larger jug, the upper handle joint is covered by a moulded shell. I am sure that some of these jugs and the leaf-moulded mugs were made before 1790 but in a contrary way some large leaf-moulded jugs were made which bear the dates 1792 and 1793, together with either initials or a name (Plate 78).

Obviously the making of presentation pieces was part of the New Hall programme. Splendid jugs, in a variety of sizes, were made with a modification of the early clip handle, some were dated and some bore initials, some were decorated

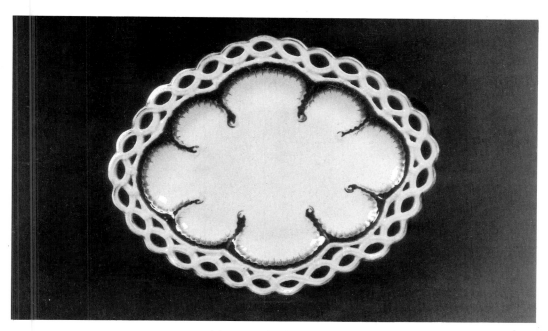

75. DESSERT-PLATE or STAND with pierced edge decorated in underglaze dark-blue and gold.
Length 26 cm (10.25 in), hard-paste, 1782–7. *See page 96.*

76. DESSERT-WARES decorated in underglaze bright-blue and gold.
Lobed dish length 22.2 cm (8.75 in), hard-paste, 1782–7. *See page 96.*

77. Leaf-moulded MUG with scroll handle
     painted in enamels (pattern 139).
     Height 9.5 cm (3.75 in), hard-paste,
     1782–7. *See page 96.*

78. Leaf-moulded JUG with scroll handle
     painted in enamels and inscribed
     'Thomas Brundrell 1793'.
     Height 17.1 cm (6.75 in), hard-paste.
     *City Museum and Art Gallery,
     Stoke-on-Trent. See page 96.*

79. JUG of high-Chelsea ewer form
     painted in enamels (pattern 20). There
     are signs of shell-moulding where the
     handle joins the rim of the jug.
     Height 7.5 cm (3 in), hard-paste,
     1782–7. *See page 96.*

80. JUG of low-Chelsea ewer form painted
     in enamels (pattern 20).
     Height 6.1 cm (2.4 in), hard-paste,
     1782–7. *See page 96.*

81. TEAPOT painted in enamels (pattern 22) and inscribed in gold:
    Whether ye eat or drink, or
    Whatsoever ye do, do all to the
    Glory of God
    John and Mary Wood
    Height 15.2 cm (6 in), hard-paste, 1785–1800. *See page 100.*

with Sadler and Green or similar prints,[11] and others, most desirable of all, were decorated by Fidelle Duvivier (see pages 118–26). These bore fine decoration but there were others made for a more mundane world which were decorated with a standard pattern and were even marked with the relevant pattern number. Although it is possible that a few of them were made in the first decade I believe that most, if not all, were made after 1790 and many about 1800.

[11]One such example was exhibited (Cat. No. 83) in the 'New Hall Bicentenary Exhibition 1781–1981' and another was shown (Cat. No. 207) in the exhibition 'English Ceramics 1580–1830' which celebrated the Fiftieth Anniversary of the English Ceramic Circle.

Dated and presentation pieces can often be used as valuable evidence in creating a chronological picture of a factory's wares. Unfortunately some pieces turn up which either topple the castle or need a special explanation. An example of this is a globular teapot which is inscribed 'Whether ye eat or drink or Whatsoever ye do, do all to the Glory of God. Johnathan and Betty Wood. 1798' in enamels.[12] The inscription was painted at the same time as the rest of the decoration. The pattern number is written beneath the pot, 'No 195', which suggests that the decoration was done at the factory. The apparent contradictions here are that the production of globular teapots is thought to be complete well before 1790 and at the time when they were made the pattern number was not put on the piece. Furthermore, it is unusual for the lid on this shape of teapot to be within the neck opening; it usually sits on top of the neck. However, since the pot was thrown on the wheel it could presumably have been made at any time. Another teapot of this shape (Plate 81) also bears this verse inscription, which is a modification of 1 Corinthians 10: 31, and the added names 'John and Mary Wood'. In this case the inscription is in gold and need not have been done at the factory. It is rather a coincidence to find both these teapots bearing the same inscription and the name of a couple called Wood. A further coincidence is that a large jug of the form mentioned in the previous paragraph is inscribed in gold 'J. & E. Wood, Padiham 1800'.[13] I am sure that there is a direct connection between these three pieces and a likely explanation is that all three were made as wedding presents, for members of the Wood family of Padiham in Lancashire. I must admit, however, that a search of the parish registers, kindly carried out for me by the Revd R. C. Hudson, has not revealed any evidence to support this theory.

Crested wares were probably made as presents. The fluted cup, with one scroll handle typical of the corrugated wares, is an interesting shape (Colour Plate H) being similar to some made at Caughley and Worcester. This fluted shape must have been used by New Hall for a brief period during the first decade for a teacup (Plate 125) decorated with pattern 3, and a round, slightly waisted teapot with this fluted moulding and the same handle form are known. Blue-and-white wares with a weaker form of this fluting have also been noted.

Chocolate-cups, or perhaps they were caudle-cups or posset-pots, are uncommon. Although they were probably made to special order, they must have been generally available since they were decorated with standard patterns. The cups had a lid and stood on a saucer with a shallow well in the bottom. The specimens with the

---

[12]David Holgate, op. cit., Plate 57.

[13]R. J. Charleston, op. cit., Plate XII.

82. COVERED CHOCOLATE-CUP with entwined-twig handles and knob, painted in enamels and gold (pattern 213).
Height 13.3 cm (5.25 in), hard-paste, 1787–90. *Godden Collection.*
See page 101.

83. COVERED POSSET-POT with entwined-twig handles painted in enamels (pattern 241).
Height 14.6 cm (5.75 in), hard-paste, 1795–1800. *See page 101.*

twisted leaf-stalk handles and knob (Plate 82) have a waisted body and are earlier than those with straight tapering sides and ring handles and a simple gilt knob (Plate 295). Since these pieces were usually decorated with gilt patterns it is possible that some are lurking in cabinets containing Chamberlain's Worcester porcelain. Bone-china examples also had straight tapering sides but typically had oval-shaped ring handles (Plate 354). On the other hand, covered bowls with entwined-twig handles and decorated with standard patterns are unmistakably New Hall (Plates 83 and 324). Occasionally after 1800 a tea-service included a covered muffin-dish (Plate 84).

New Hall flasks seem to be rare, although they must have been available throughout the hard-paste period. A large specimen in the Castle Museum, Norwich (Plate 97), probably made by combining two saucers without footrings, bears an early underglaze blue transfer-print and was made at about the same time as the smaller one, which is finely decorated in coloured enamels with a delicate spray of flowers within a pink pseudo-scale border (Colour Plate D). Another small flask, from the same mould as this latter one, decorated with a cottage scene within a

84.   COVERED MUFFIN-DISH with entwined-twig knob painted in underglaze mazarine-
       blue, enamels and gold. Enamelled mark 752.
       Diameter 19.1 cm (7.5 in), hard-paste, c. 1805. *See pages 101, 194.*

heavy gold border similar to that used for pattern 1162, being in hard-paste, was
probably made about 1812.

The present section would be incomplete without mention of the large bowls
made in both hard-paste and bone-china: bowls in sizes up to 35.5 cm (14 in) in
diameter were made. Bowls of 28 cm (11 in) diameter decorated with the 'window'
pattern (number 425)[14] are seen quite often but not so those with earlier patterns
(e.g. numbers 83[15] and 153). This size of bowl seems to have been quite deep with
rather upright sides but when the diameter was increased the sides flared outwards
suggesting use as a punch-bowl rather than a wash-basin. The decoration of these
larger bowls was often a combination of parts of several different standard patterns
and thus they were not always numbered or marked. An example decorated with an
underglaze blue transfer-print has been recorded.

Much of the interesting and unusual hard-paste porcelain was made during the
first challenging years of experimentation. By the time that the bone-china body had
become established the factory's output was standardised and reduced to a single

[14]*Northern Ceramic Society Journal*, vol. 1, 1972–3, p. 60.

[15]Cat. No. 205 of the exhibition 'English Ceramics 1580–1830' which celebrated the Fiftieth
Anniversary of the English Ceramic Circle.

style of tea-service. The prospect offered to the collector is bleak. An interest can be maintained, however, since new shapes were occasionally introduced.

Dessert-services are the best source of the unusual. Most of them feature an embossed border around the flange of the plate or the edge of the dish. This border often features a continuous flower meander (Plate 85), a rococo-style tracery with birds (Plate 86) or four different sprays of flowers with some painted or gold decoration separating them (Plate 87). The moulding may be overpainted with coloured enamels or left white on a pale-blue, pink or green ground (Colour Plate S). The central decorative motif varied and was often strikingly attractive: a basket of fruit, a bouquet of flowers or the country-house scenes which were used as pattern 984 on tea-services. Interesting and attractively shaped dishes were made as well as normal flanged plates. Heart-shaped (Plate 85) and waisted rectangular dishes were the focus of the service and sauce- or custard-tureens (Colour Plate S) sometimes completed the set.

Covered cups and bowls (Plate 324) are always interesting although frequently the covers are lost or broken. Chocolate- or caudle-cups (Plate 354) were made in bone-china using the same moulds as had been used with the earlier hard-paste body. On the other hand breakfast-sets with large cups seem to be found only in bone-china. These sets contained attractive butter- and preserve-dishes (Plate 367) which were sometimes attached to the base saucer like the dessert sauce-tureens (Colour Plate S). Unfortunately, the lids and covers are often missing.

The final sale notice of October 1835 mentions 'tea services, in a great variety of shapes and patterns'. My description of the bone-china teapots in this chapter could hardly be called a great variety of shapes. Recent research has suggested a number of new forms but, since other contemporary factories also made these shapes, more research is needed before specific distinguishing features can be given. Nothing with the New Hall concentric-rings mark has been noted and the observation that the pattern numbers used would fit most conveniently within only the New Hall pattern book is inconclusive support.

In *An Anthology of Teapots* Philip Miller illustrates three different shapes of teapot which were probably made by our factory (Plates 1778, 1779, 1839 and 1840). Two of them are decorated with pattern number 2901 and the others with patterns 2784 and 3010 respectively. There is additional and more convincing evidence for a round teapot with a dolphin-shaped handle (Plate 88) having a New Hall attribution. The milk-jug from the service containing this teapot is very similar to the one pictured with it (Plate 88). The important feature of the jug illustrated is the decoration, which uses the customary New Hall 'window' pattern outline transfer-print and palette of colours. Furthermore the jug is marked with the correct pattern number, 425.

85. DESSERT-DISH with relief-moulding
     on an underglaze pale-blue ground
     decorated with a central bat-print of
     fruit over a basket in underglaze
     mazarine-blue and gold (pattern 1478).
     Length 20.3 cm (8 in), bone-china,
     1822–35. *City Museum and Art Gallery,
     Stoke-on-Trent. See page 103.*

86. DESSERT-PLATE with relief-moulding
     and decorated with pink roses and
     green leaves in enamels on an
     underglaze pale-blue ground. The two
     underglaze mazarine-blue bands were
     overgilded. Enamelled pattern number
     1707.
     Diameter 20.3 cm (8 in), bone-china,
     1825–35. *See page 103.*

87. DESSERT-DISH with knotted-ribbon handles and relief-
     moulding on a pale-blue ground. The painted scene is in
     enamels. Enamelled pattern number 2229. Note that other
     factories made dessert-wares with knotted-ribbon handles.
     Length 28.6 cm (11.25 in), bone-china, 1825–30. *Godden
     Collection. See page 103.*

88. TEAPOT and MILK-JUG with dolphin-moulded handles. The teapot, painted in enamels, is marked with the pattern number 3639. It is probably one of the last New Hall teapot shapes. Other factories made wares of similar shape. The jug is decorated with the 'window' pattern and is marked with the correct pattern number '425' in blue.
Teapot height 15.2 cm (6 in), jug height 8.3 cm (3.25 in), bone-china, 1830–5. *Godden Collection (teapot). See page 103.*

Accepting the possibility that these teapot shapes were made at New Hall then the associated cup shapes should be noted. Contemporary factory records call the cup in Plate 91 the 'Etruscan' shape and in this example the upper part of the handle is attached to the body of the cup with a short vertical piece of clay. A saucer (Plate 92) is illustrated beside the cup in order to gain a better impression of the pattern (number 3017) which, as seems often to occur at this time, is mostly inside the cup. A cup with a gentle scallop-moulding and what is called an 'Old English' handle is shown in Plate 89 and the fluted cup which was *en suite* with the dolphin-handled teapot is shown in Plate 93. It is curious that most of these cups and their saucers bear the pattern number, a feature quite at variance with the accepted New Hall practice on the established hard-paste and bone-china wares. Whilst it is likely that these shapes were made by New Hall it must be remembered that other factories made similar shapes.

The words 'modern and fancy-shaped jugs and mugs' occur in the final sale notice of 1835 (see pages 40–1). No doubt the bone-china jugs and mugs featuring classical groups or huntsmen in bas-relief fit this description. Perhaps there is an extension to this group? Many white jugs and mugs (Plate 95, left) with applied pale-blue flowers are found. Some of these pots have a blue pad of clay impressed with the initials

89. Probably a late CUP shape made by
     New Hall.
     Height 6.2 cm (2.4 in), bone-china, c.
     1830. *See pages 90, 105.*

91. Probably a late CUP shape made by
     New Hall. Enamelled pattern number
     3017.
     Height 6.2 cm (2.4 in), bone-china, c.
     1830. *See pages 90, 105.*

90. The inside of the CUP in Plate 89 to
     show the enamel and gold decoration
     (pattern 2901).

92. SAUCER *en suite* with the cup in Plate
     91 decorated with alternate panels of
     enamelled flowers and underglaze
     mazarine-blue and gold (pattern 3017).
     Diameter 14.2 cm (5.6 in),
     bone-china, c. 1830. *See page 105.*

93. This CUP was *en suite* with the teapot in Plate 88 and is therefore probably a late New Hall product. Painted in enamels and gold (pattern 3639). Height 5.1 cm (2 in), bone-china, 1830–5. *Godden Collection. See pages 90, 105.*

94. MUG decorated in white bas-relief on a lavender-blue ground. Height 6.3 cm (2.5 in), bone-china, 1820–30. *See page 96.*

95. Two MUGS with the same moulded handle form. The mug on the right is decorated with the normal relief-moulded hunting scene overpainted with enamels. The mug on the left has applied blue flowers as decoration and is marked underneath with an applied blue scrolled pad of clay incised with the initials 'NH' (*See next page*). Height (*right*) 9.4 cm (3.7 in), 1825–35. *See pages 96, 105.*

the initials 'N H' stuck on the base. I hope that more evidence than the handle shape on this mug may be found for attributing this mark to New Hall wares.

No chimney ornaments, also mentioned in the sale notice, have yet been recorded.

CHAPTER 7

Decoration, Decorators and Marks

DECORATION

The range of decoration used by New Hall is seldom appreciated. Originally collectors recognised only the coloured sprig patterns. Later came the knowledge of the use of underglaze blue transfers. A sparing use of gold was noticed especially as a rim or edge decoration. Finally came the realisation that gold was used in both simple and elaborate designs. In fact it is known now that gold was used more frequently than any colour even from the earliest days.

When looking at the sequence of patterns we can see how the public taste changed, for the worse. The first gilt patterns were discreet and elegant (patterns 52, 83, 89), frequently showing a Meissen influence (patterns 152–5, Colour Plate J), and often a range of patterns produced by using a single basic device. For example, a narrow mazarine-blue band under the glaze could be finished with innumerable different gold lines and motifs applied over the glaze. A further modification was the replacement of the gold of a pattern by a magenta enamel; this would have been offered as a cheaper alternative. I do not know whether these variants were given a different pattern number since no pieces have been noted yet bearing a number.[1] Another range of patterns was produced with different coloured bands within two different styles of gilt border; patterns 227 (apricot) and 206 (yellow), for example, are different coloured bands within plain gold lines and these become pattern

[1] Such alternatives are known for patterns 153 and 170.

numbers 222 and 221 when black lines and a small gilt leaf-chain are added to the border. All these patterns were probably introduced before 1795.

Public taste changed as more families and a different class of people afforded a porcelain tea-set, and the style of decoration changed with it. Gilt decoration tended to cover more of the porcelain surface instead of being restricted to a simple border. Although some attractive borders were still made, e.g. gold foliage incorporating simple flowers (pattern 445 – fuchsias) or berries (pattern 291 – rose-hips), the tendency was to cover much of the surface with an underglaze dark-blue and to complete the pattern with designs in gold (patterns 581 and 779). The designer often let his imagination run riot, producing bunches of orange and blue grapes as well as natural yellow-green ones. Some of the animals used are grotesque, either intended to be like real animals, e.g. elephants and lions (patterns 1054 and 1214), which the decorator had probably never seen in real life, or else perhaps of heraldic or mythological origin (pattern 550).

In the bone-china period, gold was used with more discretion. Generally it would seem that its use was to complete a pattern rather than form a main part of it. The white body was seemingly more suited to bright colours than gold. However, towards the end of the factory's life, perhaps about 1825, some all-over brightly coloured patterns in an Imari style were heightened or weighted by the addition of gold.

Silver lustre was used as part of a few patterns. Since none of these was given a number they cannot be placed exactly in the pattern book. Most of them appear on services featuring the boat-shaped teapot and the hard-paste cups have the enclosed ring handle (Plate 96). It is likely that these pieces were made at the beginning of the nineteenth century.

By accident or design – probably the latter – when New Hall began they used coloured decoration from a palette whose range of bright, clean colours was excellent. The most likely reason for this is the wealth of experience and knowledge within the Warburton family. It is most likely that the factory had its own decorating shop from the earliest days at Shelton Hall, and this would be a bold innovation. Many Staffordshire potters used to send their wares to special decorating shops – like Ann Warburton's – and few before New Hall decorated on the premises in their own studio.

Throughout the hard-paste period the general style of enamel decoration was remarkably constant: only the quality and artistic merit changed. The patterns are taken almost universally as being typical New Hall decoration. The simple borders were endless variations on the use of dots, lines, blobs and garlands, whilst the main design was a collection of flowers. Few of the flowers have parallels in nature but

96.   TEACUP decorated mainly with silver lustre. No pattern number appears to have been
given to patterns using this style of decoration.
Height 5.6 cm (2.25 in), hard-paste, 1800–12. *See page 110.*

this does not seem to affect the pleasing, naïve effect. Of course, these borders and
sprays were not truly original designs, they merely reflected the style of
contemporary ornament and decoration. Many of the simple borders are similar to
the engraving on silver tea-wares. Printed patterns were available for needlework
samplers which had borders of rosebuds and anthemia, and featured sprays or
baskets of flowers.

During the first decade very attractive polychrome patterns were used. These
were mostly neat and of almost realistic flower sprays beneath a simple border (e.g.
patterns 3 and 139) but a few chinoiserie designs are known (patterns 20 and 157).

The use of yellow and blue enamels at this time is worth noting because neither
was a very easy colour to apply. In fact they soon disappeared from the palette and
although they returned at a later date their colour was relatively poor and lifeless.
The problem with blue enamel is its lack of opacity. A normal thickness of blue
enamel does not obliterate the background and a thicker layer is needed. This extra
thickness of enamel, however, readily chips off the glaze – a fault which occurs
frequently with the blue border on pieces decorated with pattern 22.

The early polychrome patterns were very popular and many of them had a long life, e.g. 171 and 186, which are found on tea-sets made throughout the hard-paste period as well as on bone-china services. As time went by the neatness and rhythm of the flower sprays diminished, and this again was probably a reflection of the public taste. By varying the colour of the border used for a given spray the number of different patterns was increased without much extra effort on the part of the designer. Thus we find two borders with the same sprays (patterns 746 and 791). It is rather confusing, though, to find in one case two different monochrome and one polychrome versions of a pattern given different numbers (367, 598, 599) whilst in another case only one number, 241, is given to the polychrome and the black monochrome versions of a single pattern. This must have caused difficulty and uncertainty at the factory if someone wanted extra pieces made to replace broken ones.

No doubt an attempt was made in the bone-china period to cater for different tastes and pockets. On the one hand we find perfunctory decoration (pattern 1084) and simple borders and on the other hand all-over designs, often on a powder-blue background, featuring mazarine-blue leaves outlined and decorated with gold, and flowers and ornaments washed in with orange colour (pattern 1373). Another variety of decoration featured bat-printed[2] sprays of flowers, or birds, washed over with coloured enamels (patterns 1511 and 1560). At its best the decoration was very attractive showing considerable artistic merit.

It is no surprise to find extensive use made of transfer- and bat-printing processes. How could a factory function successfully during the period 1781 to 1835 without taking advantage of the repetitive techniques which increased the speed and economy of reproducing a given design?

Underglaze blue transfer-decoration was successfully applied to the hard-paste porcelain from the earliest days. It was a considerable achievement, since Plymouth and Bristol had been unsuccessful. The different firing schedule and manufacturing method developed by these Staffordshire potters created a suitably hard biscuit body to receive the transfer-print. However, the temperature needed for maturing the glaze, as well as its composition, did not really suit the cobalt-blue. At no time was the final colour comparable to the best product of the soft-paste factories.

The patterns were mostly of a willow-pattern type with Chinese pagodas, willow-trees (Plate 103), a bridge with a man on it (Plate 100) and various types of boats. Other designs feature a pair of moth-like flying insects (Plate 104), swimming

---

[2]Bat-printing is a process of printing from engraved copper plates (usually stippled) in which a bat of gelatine takes the place of a transfer-tissue.

97. FLASK decorated with underglaze blue transfer-print. The reverse side of this flask has the transfer-print shown in Plate 98.
Height 12.7 cm (5 in), hard-paste, 1782–7. *Norfolk Museums Service, Castle Museum, Norwich. See pages 101, 116.*

99. PICKLE-DISH decorated with the underglaze blue transfer-print referred to as the 'gazebo' pattern.
Length 17 cm (6.7 in), hard-paste, 1782–7. *See pages 96, 116.*

98. CUP decorated with underglaze blue transfer-print.
Height 6.6 cm (2.6 in), hard-paste, 1782–7. *See page 116.*

100. TEAPOT decorated with underglaze blue transfer-print and gold. The ring knob is uncommon.
Height 17 cm (6.7 in), hard-paste, *Godden Collection. See pages 51(n. 2), 112.*

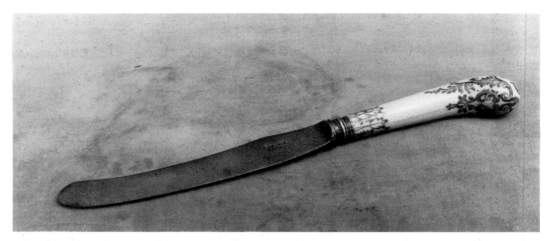

101. KNIFE with a porcelain handle decorated with underglaze blue transfer-print. Length (handle) 8.6 cm (3.4 in), hard-paste, 1782–7. *See page 96.*

102. SAUCER decorated with underglaze blue transfer-print and gold. Diameter 12.7 cm (5 in), hard-paste, 1785–1800. *See page 116.*

103. SAUCER decorated with underglaze blue transfer-print and gold. Diameter 12.7 cm (5 in), hard-paste, 1782–95. *See page 112.*

104. PLATE decorated with underglaze blue transfer-print. Diameter 21.6 cm (8.5 in), hard-paste, 1790–1810. *See page 112.*

106. Three-footed JUG hand-painted in underglaze blue. Height 12 cm (4.75 in), hard-paste, 1782–7. *Godden Collection. See pages 80, 116.*

105. PLATE decorated with underglaze blue transfer-print. Diameter 21.1 cm (8.3 in), hard-paste, 1800–10. *See page 116.*

107. ASPARAGUS-SERVER decorated with underglaze blue transfer-print. Length 8.1 cm (3.2 in), hard-paste, 1782–7. *See page 96.*

ducks (Plate 105) and a row of 'drainpipes' (Plate 102) which Dr Watney has likened to trench mortars.[3] Two of the rarer designs show children playing – a delightful scene – and a flowering shrub with two flying doves above it. The former seems to feature two different scenes. Two figures by an obelisk, which is found on teapots, saucers and a flask (Plate 97), and two figures by a small thatched well, which is found on jugs and cups (Plate 98). The latter design is coupled with a willow-root and other pieces of the flowering shrub (Colour Plate G). One of the most interesting patterns incorporates a pagoda in a cleft rock (commonly called a gazebo). Rare pieces like leaf-shaped pickle-trays (Plate 99) have been found bearing this decoration, as well as a tea-service whose teapot, sucrier and jug bore the crowned lion mark.[4]

Most of the borders, like those commonly found with willow patterns, are uninspired and also hard to distinguish. But one of overlapping pointed leaves which appears with the gazebo pattern (Plate 99) and another with trefoil-shaped leaves hanging from the line border (Colour Plate G) are simple enough to be pleasing.

These blue transfer-prints were used almost throughout the hard-paste period, for they are found applied to the majority of the different shapes, e.g. globular, silver-shape, boat-shaped, oval-based straight-sided and waisted teapots. However, the real collector's interest is focused on the early pieces like the asparagus-servers, knife-handles and leaf-dishes, and so far these pieces have been found only with underglaze blue decoration. It must also be noted that a few pieces were decorated with hand-painted underglaze blue decoration (Plate 106) and here the blue is somewhat brighter and cleaner since none of the additives needed for printing would have been used.

The public demand for blue-and-white transfer-printed porcelain tea-sets declined with the onset of the nineteenth century. By this time there were few New Hall tea-sets made with this decoration and no new designs were created. However, a few bone-china services have been noted, but these, since they were decorated with a form of the common 'Brosely' pattern or a typical Miles Mason print,[5] were possibly decorated using transfers or plates acquired from other factories. Some underglaze transfers were used as outlines for overglaze decoration. Several different

---

[3]Robert Copeland has recommended that the design be named 'Malayan Village' due to the close resemblance to a scene in Daniell's *Picturesque Voyage to India by way of China* (E.C.C. *Trans.*, vol. 10, part 2, 1977, p. 100).

[4]Part of this service is illustrated in David Holgate, *New Hall and Its Imitators*, 1971, Plate 185.

[5]R. Haggar and E. Adams, *Mason Porcelain and Ironstone 1796–1853*, 1977, Plate 49.

K. TEAPOT of silver-shape decorated in enamels with a
scene of 'Minster Abbey' taken from an engraving
in Samuel Ireland's *Picturesque Views on the River
Medway* (Plate 128) published in 1793.
Height 15 cm (5.9 in), hard-paste, 1793–5.
Godden Collection.

L. TEA-WARES painted in enamels and gold. The two covered sucriers and the spoon-tray
are decorated with pattern 83, the tea-caddy with pattern 89.
Spoon-tray length 14.6 cm (5.75 in), tea-caddy height 12.7 cm (5 in), hard-paste,
1785–95. *See pages 85, 94, 95.*

M. COFFEE-POT painted in enamels (pattern 297).
Height 25 cm (9.8 in), hard-paste, c. 1795. *See page 70.*

N. TEA-WARES featuring an 'old oval shape' teapot. The basic pattern was used with several different combinations of colours; this one, in underglaze mazarine-blue completed with enamels and gold, is pattern 490.
Teapot height 16 cm (6.3 in), hard-paste, c. 1800. *See pages 85, 117.*

O. PRESENTATION JUG with a scroll clip handle. The decoration is a well-painted bouquet of flowers in enamels and the monogram 'TC' in gold.
Height 19.7 cm (7.75 in), hard–paste, c. 1800.
Luton Museum and Art Gallery. See pages 51, 78, 126.

P. WATER-JUG decorated in enamels with ears of barley within a circle of leaves and the inscription 'John Brown, Yoxall, 1811' in gold. This is an important documentary jug which suggests that hard-paste was still being made in 1811.

Height 13.5 cm (5.3 in), hard-paste. *Godden Collection. See pages 48, 80.*

Q. TEAPOT of London-shape decorated with a bat-print of a 'mother and child' scene overpainted with enamels (pattern 1277). These scenes were inspired by the engravings of Adam Buck.
Height 15.3 cm (6 in), bone-china, 1815–25. *See Plate 109 and pages 50, 64, 118.*

R. TEAPOT of London-shape with the later more angular handle shape. The band of roses painted in enamels and gold is between two typical underglaze mazarine-blue and gold narrow borders (pattern 1865).
Height 15.5 cm (6.1 in), bone-china, 1820–30. *See pages 50, 66.*

S. Bone-china DESSERT-WARES. The three plates show the different coloured grounds which were used behind the white moulded-flower border. The covered sauce-tureen has the moulded-flower border picked out in enamels. The blue-ground plate is pattern 1478, the green-ground plate is pattern 1506 and the pink-ground plate which has the mark 'New Hall' within two concentric rings is pattern 1480.
Sauce-tureen height 15 cm (5.9 in), 1820–30.
City Museum and Art Gallery, Stoke-on-Trent. See page 103.

versions of the same pattern could then be marketed by adding different colour combinations (patterns 272, 274, 360, 490 (Colour Plate N) and 856).

On-glaze transfers were used to outline the Chinese courtyard scenes (patterns 425 and 621) and these were completed with enamel colours. When bat-printing was introduced, about 1800, a more detailed picture could be applied to the glaze and New Hall quickly began to use the new process (pattern 462). Later the pictures were coloured. Realistic country scenes, some actually named, were depicted and a tea-set would show several scenes (pattern 984). It is possible that many of these were taken from engravings since, for example, the scene named 'Cusworth' (Plate

108.   SAUCER decorated with a black bat-print named 'Cusworth' (pattern 1063). Diameter 14 cm (5.5 in), bone-china, 1815–20. *See page 117.*

108) appears in a book of topographical prints published in 1807 by W. Angus.[6] The name 'harlequin set' has been given to these series of prints. Various gilt borders were used to complete the decoration and these gave rise to different pattern numbers.

In 1810, Peter Warburton took out a patent for a method of printing these landscapes and country scenes in gold and platinum instead of the commonly used black. This decoration produces a handsome effect since the gold has usually mellowed beautifully. Mazarine-blue borders with added gilt decoration were sometimes added but this can make the whole effect rather heavy.

On bone-china a popular series of printed patterns was inspired by engravings designed by Adam Buck, the society portrait painter who exhibited frequently in the Royal Academy exhibitions from 1795 until his death in 1833. Different scenes of a mother and her child are depicted but very few, if any, can actually be related directly to a Buck original. Probably the engraver had seen some of Buck's work (e.g. Plate 109) and then modified the theme (Plate 63). The prints are found in black alone (pattern 1109) and with the print colour-washed over (patterns 1236 and 1525). The latter variant sometimes has added gold decoration and sometimes is a vignette within a mazarine-blue background (Colour Plate Q). These variations provided the customer with a wide price range from which to choose.

DECORATORS

The simplicity and straightforward nature of the greater part of New Hall's decoration enabled a painter of ordinary skill to be employed as a decorator. Little artistic genius was needed beyond the ability to copy. It is not surprising then that the work of individual painters has not been recognised and signed pieces are at a premium. Anonymity is the fate of the painters who worked in the New Hall studio.

Fidelle Duvivier is the only painter whose work has been identified. He was possibly responsible for creating the patterns used during the first decade. Born in Tournai in 1740 and learning his craft there, he spent most of his life decorating English porcelain. Besides working in London and at Worcester he is known to have been employed by William Duesbury for four years from 1769. Whilst he was

---

[6] *Seats of the Nobility and Gentry in Great Britain and Wales from Pictures and Drawings by the most Eminent Artists and Descriptions of each View.*

How well indulgent Nature knows,
The weight each Body bears;
See Childhood scarce supported goes,
Dismissing half its fears.

STEP BY STEP,
OR
THE PROGRESS OF HUMAN LIFE.

Fresh strength the Urchin daily proves,
Till with a Warriors stride,
O'er Realms in arms Man fiercely moves,
Creation's Shame or Pride.

109. Engraving entitled 'STEP BY STEP or THE PROGRESS OF HUMAN LIFE' from a drawing by Adam Buck. It has the verse:

How well indulgent Nature knows,
   The weight each Body bears;
See Childhood scarce supported goes,
   Dismissing half its fears.

Fresh strength the Urchin daily proves,
   Till with a Warriors stride,
O'er Realms in arms Man fiercely moves,
   Creation's Shame or Pride.

C.J.

Inscribed: 'Adam Buck, del.' 'Rob.ᵗ Cooper, sculp.' 'London Pub. 2ᵈ Janʸ 1809, at R. Ackermann's Repository of Arts 101, Strand.'

working at Derby his son Peter Joseph was born: he was baptised there on 20 March 1771. In 1790 he wrote to William Duesbury:

> Hanley green, the 1 novebr 1790, Mr Dousbery, Sir, – take the liberty Adressing you with a few lines, as mine engegement in the new Hal Porcelaine manufatory is Expierd, and the propriotors do not intend to do much more in the fine line of Painting, therefor think of Settling in new Castle under lime being engag'd to teech Drowing in the Boarding School at that place, one School I have at Stone, so as to have only three days to Spare in the week for Painting, which time Could wish to be employ'd by you preferable to eany other fabricque, because you like and understand good work, as am inform'd, my painting now, to watt I did for your father, is quit diferent but without flattering my Self, Hope to give you Satisfaction, in Case you Schould like to inploy me, Sir, – your anser will much oblige your Humble Servant, Duvivier.
>
> P.S. the conveyance would be much in fevoir for to Send the ware to and from, as ther is a waggon Every week from darby to new Castle.

This letter quoted by Jewitt[7] is important since it proves that Duvivier worked at New Hall and was about to leave there in 1790. The comment 'do not intend to do much more in the fine line of Painting' is significant since by the date of this letter the simplified and streamlined range of potting shapes and with it, presumably, the style of decoration, had been introduced.

The ascription of certain New Hall wares to this painter is based on grounds of style observable on five signed items. A Worcester teapot (in the Ashmolean Museum, Oxford), the 'Gerverot beaker',[8] and three New Hall pieces: a clip-handled cup in the Luton Museum Art Gallery (Plate 110) bearing the signature *F:. Duvivier fecir* , a tankard in the Victoria and Albert Museum (Plate 113) and a bowl in the British Museum, previously attributed to John Turner[9] but in my opinion made by New Hall. Whilst it is likely that more porcelain decorated by Duvivier will be discovered it has been shown that at least ten New Hall services painted in coloured enamels and eight in sepia monochrome were made.[10] The

[7] Ll. Jewitt, op. cit., vol. 2, p. 97.

[8] B. Hillier, op. cit., Frontispiece and Plate 34b.

[9] B. Hillier, op. cit., Plate 34c.

[10] E.C.C. Trans., vol. 11, part 1, 1981, pp. 12–20.

110. The 'Fox and Stork' fable painted in enamels and gold by Fidelle Duvivier on a signed clip-handled CUP. Height 6.1 cm (2.4 in), hard-paste, 1782–7. *Luton Museum and Art Gallery. See page 120.*

111. Clip-handled CUP painted with a river scene in enamels and gold by Fidelle Duvivier. Height 6.1 cm (2.4 in), hard-paste, 1782–7. *Victoria and Albert Museum. See page 125.*

112. Three CUPS with groove handles painted with children in enamels and gold by Fidelle Duvivier. Height 6.3 cm (2.5 in), hard-paste, 1782–7. *Luton Museum and Art Gallery. See page 125.*

113.   MUG with loop handle painted in enamels and gold with an outdoor convivial scene
by Fidelle Duvivier. It is signed twice, 'Duvivier pinx' and 'Duvivier'.
Height 9.1 cm (3.6 in), hard-paste, 1782–7. *Victoria and Albert Museum. See pages 120,
125.*

114. WATER-JUG painted in enamels and gold by Fidelle Duvivier. This jug was probably painted by Duvivier after his contract with the factory had been terminated since the shape of the jug suggests a date of 1800–10.
Height 20.4 cm (8 in), hard-paste, 1800–10. *Recreational Services: Usher Gallery, Lincoln. See pages 125, 126.*

115.   COVERED SUCRIER painted on the
body with cupids and on the lid with
trophies in enamels and gold by
Fidelle Duvivier.
Height 10.5 cm (4.1 in), hard-paste,
1782–90. *Godden Collection.*
See page 125.

116.   TEA-CADDY painted in sepia enamels
by Fidelle Duvivier.
Height 14 cm (5.5 in), hard-paste,
1782–7. *See pages 94, 125.*

117.   Clip-handled CUP featuring a smoking kiln painted in sepia
enamels with a gold rim by Fidelle Duvivier.
Height 6.1 cm (2.4 in), hard-paste, 1782–7. *See page 126.*

118. SAUCER decorated with figures in a landscape featuring a windmill in sepia enamel within a gold border by Fidelle Duvivier.
Diameter 13 cm (5.1 in), hard-paste, 1782–7. *See page 125.*

subjects seem to fall into four categories: full-sized figures of people,[11] cupids (Plate 115), children (Plate 112) or revellers in front of an inn (Plate 113), boat-scenes (Plate 111),[12] birds on rocks (Colour Plate F), and outlined figures in rural landscapes (Colour Plates E and F, Plates 114, 116, 118). This last group seems to be the most numerous. The illustrations show clearly several characteristics of the artist's style, in particular the delicate outlining of the small figures and houses which are set in rural scenes. In spite of the minute size of these figures they are full of character and their dress is clearly recognisable as the fashion of the day. The horses in particular are skilfully and occasionally amusingly drawn; sometimes they seem to sag under the weight of their rider and at others delicately crop the grass while waiting for a

[11]Where the figures are the principal feature of the decoration they appear to have embryonic-sized heads and heavy forearms with podgy hands.

[12]While the cup in Plate 111 shows three men rowing across a river, the more common scene, which is also on the other side of this cup, depicts larger ships, often with furled sails and being unloaded. R. J. Charleston, op. cit., Plate 61B.

master; or else they are pulling the common stage-coach away into the distance showing a fine rear-end view of both horse and wagon! Long-backed hounds may accompany the horse or arrive on the scene to join a conversation piece. The handling of the background in which the hazy distance fades delicately into the grey sky is reminiscent of early water-colours. The gable ends and fenestration of the cottages, the windmills, often without sails, recall Duvivier's European upbringing, whilst the smoking kilns (Plate 117) are part of his adopted life.

It is difficult to know whether Duvivier's different decorations were given numbers in the pattern book. The two pieces so far known which bear numbers (5 and 7) have different blue-and-gold borders as well as different types of decoration. I think it is likely that these borders and not the scenes would be related to the numbers.

Although all these Duvivier-decorated pieces were made before 1790, the date of the letter to Duesbury, they hardly constitute nine years' work. What else did Duvivier do at New Hall? Possibly he designed some of the early patterns, he may even have painted some of them, but it seems to me unlikely that he would do much repetitive work. I think that it is quite possible that he was never fully occupied at the factory and that the letter to Duesbury should be interpreted to mean that he was only employed for three days a week at New Hall and had been working as a drawing master for some years.

About the turn of the century New Hall made a number of presentation jugs (Colour Plate O). Most have gold initials added and a few are dated.[13] The style of the flower decoration on these jugs is remarkably consistent and suggests a single artist, but one who may not have been fully employed by the factory. Besides painting these jugs he was also responsible for the flowers painted on a few tea-services (patterns 426 and 611 are two examples). The presence of kidney-shaped petals on some of the flowers is a typical feature and an orange chrysanthemum-like flower is commonly found.

There are two important presentation jugs in the collections of the City of Stoke-on-Trent Museum and one in the Usher Art Gallery, Lincoln (Plate 114), which were probably painted by Fidelle Duvivier and, if so, as an outside decorator. One of these,[14] with a bird and its nest on one side, is illustrated by Jewitt, who states that the initials 'S.D.' were those of Samuel Daniel, a cousin of John Daniel, one of the partners.

[13]R. J. Charleston, op. cit., Colour Plate XII, inscribed 'J. and E. Wood, Padiham, 1800'.

[14]Ll. Jewitt, op. cit., vol. 2, p. 97. Illustrated in David Holgate, 1971, *New Hall and Its Imitators*, Plate 13 and *E.C.C. Trans.*, vol. 11, part 1, 1981, Plate 14 (a and b).

F. H. Rhead[15] names the three artists Henry Bone, Thomas Pardoe and Joshua Christall as decorating New Hall porcelain but no further confirmatory evidence has been found. In fact apart from Duvivier no New Hall decorator has been positively identified, nor does there seem room for them.

MARKS

There was no factory mark during the hard-paste period. The occurrence of on-glaze Sèvres, Plymouth and Bristol marks is misleading and in many cases faked. Two tea-bowls in the Victoria and Albert Museum (pattern 153) have the Sèvres mark ⚭ in a bright-blue colour which is atypical and the date in a gold whose soft easily-rubbed nature is different from the main gilt decoration. Also in the Victoria and Albert Museum are a coffee-cup and saucer both bearing a blue cross mark. The cup was made at New Hall (pattern 195) and the saucer was made by another factory and decorated with their version of the pattern! No doubt the mark was intended to seal the marriage of the two pieces and to ensure that they should live in a 'Bristol' cabinet.

Pattern numbers are the only regularly used marks which have been noted. These are found alone or accompanied by the letters 'N' or 'No'. The colour used is chosen quite arbitrarily and is not necessarily found in the pattern itself. This suggests that someone may have been deputed to put these numbers on the pieces, either before decoration to instruct the painter or after the painting to help the sorters assemble the orders. These numbers are found under the principal pieces of a service, i.e. teapot and stand, sugar-bowl, jug, basins and plates but never regularly under the tea-bowls, cups or saucers. In fact, the number of these latter pieces which bear a pattern number is so small that they constitute exceptions which prove the rule. It should be borne in mind that in the years of experimentation even these pattern numbers were rarely used. Their introduction was delayed until the late 1780s.

A few of the early blue-and-white pieces were marked with a crowned lion

---

[15]*Connoisseur*, September 1916, p. 221.

mark[16] under the glaze, but this mark was not used regularly. It would seem that the underglaze transfer-prints were not usually allotted a pattern number although a few pieces have been noted with the numbers 473 and 604. However, the application of these numbers to a specific transfer-print or a particular gold embellishment is not consistent and further research is needed before a reliable statement can be made.

Frequently painters' marks are found but they are unreliable guides to identification. However, it has been suggested[17] that three of these marks are typical. They are generally found on pieces made towards the end of the hard-paste period. The 'f' mark is also found on some of the early bone-china pieces.

The names of two different retailers have been noted painted in on-glaze enamel on the inside of the lids of teapots and sucriers. Since the teapots were of the larger boat-shape they would have been made probably after 1800. The retailers were Elijah Cotton of Edinburgh and Abbott and Mist of Fleet Street, London.

During the bone-china period a factory identification mark was used. This was a transfer-print of two concentric rings surrounding the words 'New Hall' in script. Sometimes it accompanied the pattern number on the important pieces of a service but more frequently it was applied to the saucers. Jewitt[18] suggests that it was introduced after 1820 and used sparingly but since it is found beneath many pieces decorated with early bone-china patterns (e.g. pattern 1109) the date of introduction was more likely to be 1815. Moreover, I am not convinced that 'sparingly' really describes its use.

A rare mark which I have seen only beneath a bone-china dessert-plate has '*Newhall*' in continuous script without the circles. A reported variation of this mark divides the name into two words.[19]

It is possible that in the last five years of production some jugs and mugs with applied blue decoration and with a distinctive mark on the base were made at New

---

[16]Roger Pomfret has suggested to me in private correspondence and discussion the possibility that the lion-marked pieces were made by John Turner in partnership with Louis-Victor Gerverot (Bevis Hillier, op. cit., pp. 40–5). A whiter body, brownish translucency, glaze imperfections within the footring, more sharply defined, wider-spaced line-engravings and a round knob on teapot, jug and caddy-lids being frequent features on marked pieces. On the other hand, my wife, whose specialism is John Turner, believes that this group of blue-and-white wares was made during the brief time at Keeling's factory when Richard Champion and John Turner were part of the original New Hall partnership (*Northern Ceramic Society Journal*, vol. 6, 1987).

[17]R. J. Charleston, op. cit., p. 159.

[18]Ll. Jewitt, op. cit., vol. 2, p. 97.

[19]On a bone-china dessert-plate in the Maidstone Museum and Art Gallery.

Hall. This mark was a raised pad of blue clay with the impressed initials 'N H' within the scroll outline (see page 108).

Finally I must mention an impressed mark of 'NEWHALL'. This is found beneath smear-glazed stoneware pieces, redware and probably earthenware made by Thomas Booth and Sons, who worked in part of the New Hall premises between 1872 and 1880. A teapot with this mark is in the Harris Museum, Preston and a jug in Canada has a registration mark giving 1867 as the date of registration of the pattern, besides the name of the manufactory.

MARKS

The crowned lion mark
(*see footnote 16, page 128*)

The mark found on a few pieces of tea-services decorated with stipple prints in gold

Bone-china marks

Workmen's marks

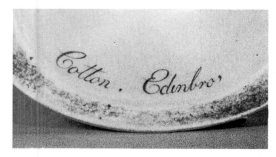

Retailers' marks

NEWHALL

Impressed mark and Patent Office Registration mark sometimes found on pieces made by Thomas Booth c. 1872–80.

CHAPTER 8

Traps for the Unwary

New Hall had the protection of Champion's patent from a potter who might wish to use china-clay and china-stone to make porcelain. On the other hand, there was no such protection from anyone who wanted to make tea-wares which looked like theirs. Anyone could make a silver-shape teapot, anyone could decorate a tea-bowl with a 'red ribbon' border or a 'basket of flowers'; several potters did. Perhaps Hollins, Warburton, Daniel and Company were flattered, no doubt their eighteenth-century customer was content; the twentieth-century collector is plagued and beset by the problems of identification which they cause. The possibility of finding a piece of porcelain wrongly attributed is probably greater in the case of New Hall than for any other eighteenth-century factory. How then are the pitfalls to be avoided, even eliminated?

Firstly, little reliance should be put on decoration. By all means be attracted by the pattern but then be suspicious and look for other evidence. Should you be looking at a plain tea-bowl or a saucer there is little help forthcoming unless you are very experienced in the appearance of the glaze, its sheen or the gas bubbles within it. On the other hand if the object is a larger piece of tea-ware such as a teapot or a plate then there will probably be a pattern number on the underside. Assuming that the correct pattern and its number are associated then you can feel more confident in identifying the maker; for instance, if the decoration is the 'red ribbon' pattern and the number on the pot is 186 then New Hall was the maker, but if the number is 116 or 126 then it was not. Again, the 'shell' pattern, number 1045 in the New Hall pattern book, was used by other factories as number 29 or 811. New Hall's pattern

195 was used by at least six other potters and given the numbers 2 (Turner), 7 (Minton), 124, 125, 145 and 189 (Herculaneum).

The only sure way to identify a piece is by its shape. Despite there being no copyright for shape we can nevertheless distinguish one factory's ware from another's. This is because moulds were needed to make the pots and no two factories used identical moulds. Thus all teapots made from a New Hall mould look alike and yet are different in detail from those of any other factory which sought to use a similar shape. It is only by very careful attention to detail that one can distinguish New Hall from its imitators. For instance, a collector inspecting a teapot must study the details of any applied moulding, the shape of the spout and handle, the knob on the lid, or the base upon which the pot stands.

Spiral- or S-shape fluting (called by some eighteenth-century manufacturers shanking or shankering) is the simplest example to use (Plate 119). Different factories used different radii for the curves; some used gentle curves and some sharp, sometimes the two curves had the same radius, sometimes not and sometimes the spines or ridges were sharp and well defined whilst on others they were scarcely discernible. New Hall used curves of equal radius and the flutes were shallow. The effect is leisurely and discreet. In the case of tea-bowls and cups the top end of each individual curve is aligned with the bottom end. When this kind of fluting is used on New Hall silver-shape teapots the vertical columns on each side remain straight and upright (Plate 19) but on the examples of at least one other factory (Plate 121) they follow the line of the curves and the teapot looks as though it is ready to fall forward.

When considering a silver-shape teapot a first indication can be gained from the proportion of height to length. However, the best clues come from the way the top of the handle is attached to the teapot body and from the sinuous curves of the spout. Although the top fastening of a New Hall handle was V-shape on the early specimens and U-shape on the later standard examples, they always overlapped the body by at least a centimetre. The handle applied by one other factory, that most commonly found, hardly overlaps the body at all and often bends forward towards the collar opening before looping back and downwards (Plate 120). The principal distinguishing feature of a teapot spout is the curve of the upper edge. In the examples shown in Plates 120 and 121 it is obvious that the curves of the upper and lower edges follow each other whilst the upper edge of a New Hall teapot spout is almost straight.

In a similar way a close study of the potting features of jugs can identify the New Hall specimens. Plate 122 indicates clearly how the general proportions of silver-shape jugs can differ and how the handles may be attached to the body of the jug in a

119. Three spiral-fluted CUPS decorated in enamels and, on the left, with gold. The centre cup is New Hall (pattern 267). The fluting on the two outer cups is much more sharply defined than on the New Hall cup and their handles are quite different from any used by New Hall.

Centre cup height 7 cm (2.75 in), all are hard-paste and 1795–1805. *See page 132.*

120. Silver-shape TEAPOT with reeded moulding and decorated in enamels. Not New Hall. Note the shape of the spout and the way the handle joins the body.

Height 15.2 cm (6 in), hard-paste, 1796–1805. *See page 132.*

121. Silver-shape TEAPOT with applied curved fluting, moulded strawberry knob and painted in enamels. Enamelled pattern number 105. Note the shape of the spout and compare this and the fluting with the New Hall example in Plate 19. Not New Hall. Height 14 cm (5.5 in), hard-paste, 1796–1805. *See pages 59, 132.*

122. Three silver-shape JUGS. Jug (*left*) is New Hall painted in sepia enamel and gold and with enamelled pattern number 285; jug (*centre*) is painted in enamels and with enamelled pattern number 231; jug (*right*) painted in enamels. Note the different proportions of the bodies, curves of the spouts and shapes of the handles. Jug (*left*) height 10.8 cm (4.25 in), all are hard-paste and 1795–1805. *Godden Collection. See page 132.*

123. Two JUGS painted in enamels. The ridge on both handles and the sharpness of the
     fluting on the left jug establish that they are not New Hall.
     Height of both 12.7 cm (5 in), both are hard-paste and 1796–1805. *Godden Collection.*
     See page 136.

124. Three obconical JUGS painted in enamels. Only the one on the right is New Hall.
     The jug (*centre*) is decorated with New Hall's pattern 195 but is marked in enamel
     '124'. Its shape should be compared with the New Hall jug in Plate 40.
     Height of the New Hall jug on the right 11.4 cm (4.5 in), all are hard-paste and
     1790–1800. *Godden Collection. See page 136.*

different place on different examples. Similarly, helmet-shaped and obconical jugs also can be distinguished. In Chapter 6 the potting features of New Hall specimens have been described and the collector must be suspicious of a jug with any novel features. Whilst the jugs shown in Plate 123 have a different general shape from New Hall examples the ridge on the handle sets them apart. On New Hall helmet-shaped jugs the only commonly applied handle-feature is the clip. The obconical jugs in Plate 124 also differ significantly in shape from New Hall specimens. An interesting feature of these jugs is the way in which the pattern number is written. The number '124' under the jug in the centre is written neatly in iron-red and has a small 'x' beside the number. From my experience and observation there appears to be one potter who made tea-sets featuring silver-shape teapots and obconical jugs and marked them in this way, with a number and an 'x'. Unlike New Hall's, the coffee-cups, tea-bowls and saucers were also similarly marked. The pattern number beneath the jug on the left is written so that it faces outwards towards the rim. Now almost all factories, and New Hall in particular, wrote the pattern numbers facing towards the centre, in the same way as the numbers on old clock-dials. I imagine that from the decorator's view-point the difference is that most painters held the pot and put the number at the top of the piece but at this factory he painted the number at the bottom.

Only cautious use should be made of these observations; they should be used as a guide only, for I am sure that there are exceptions. There may have been a number of occasions when a New Hall decorator put the number in an unaccustomed place or decided to put an 'x' after it.

The habit of tea-drinking became common throughout society by the beginning of the nineteenth century so that many potters must have been tempted to make porcelain tea-sets. They would start only in a small way, some never getting beyond this stage, and would not employ special designers and decorators. Thus they would naturally use shapes and patterns which were currently popular. Why not? They were not out to start a new fashion necessarily or build a new factory, merely to extend their business and make a small profit. They were not necessarily consciously imitating New Hall (or any other factory for that matter) merely following fashion. More truthfully then it is not a case of 'New Hall and Its Imitators' but rather New Hall and its contemporaries.

I hope that these comments will help collectors and students to avoid adding unwanted pieces to their New Hall collections. In my previous book I discussed some known factories which made and decorated teawares in a similar style to New Hall and I drew attention to three groups of similar wares whose makers were unknown. In doing this I hoped that some marked pieces might materialise and thus the makers would be identified. So far this hope has not been fulfilled; in fact more groups have been established! However, books have been published now on a number of individual, named, factories like Miles Mason and Chamberlain at Worcester, as well as research papers and a general book which expands considerably our knowledge of the wares of the unidentified potters. I commend the following publications to the interested reader:

Michael Berthoud, *An Anthology of British Cups*, Wingham, 1982.

Geoffrey Godden, *Minton Pottery and Porcelain of the First Period, 1793–1850*, London, 1968.

Geoffrey Godden, *Coalport and Coalbrookdale Porcelains*, London, 1970.

Geoffrey Godden, *The Illustrated Guide to Ridgway Porcelains*, London, 1972.

Geoffrey Godden, *Chamberlain and Worcester Porcelain, 1788–1855*, London, 1982.

Geoffrey Godden (Editor), *Staffordshire Porcelain*, London, 1983.

R. G. Haggar and E. Adams, *Mason Porcelain and Ironstone, 1796–1853*, London, 1977.

T. A. Lockett, *Davenport Pottery and Porcelain, 1794–1887*, Newton Abbot, 1972.

Philip Miller and Michael Berthoud, *An Anthology of British Teapots*, Wingham, 1985.

A. Smith, *The Illustrated Guide to Liverpool Herculaneum Pottery*, London, 1970.

L. Whiter, *Spode: A History of the Family, Factory and Wares from 1733–1833*, London, 1970.

Articles in the *Northern Ceramic Society Journal*, vols. 1–4, 1972–3, 1975–6, 1978–9, 1980–1, on Davenport, the Factories X, Y and Z, Neale, Machin, Minton and New Hall.

CHAPTER 9

A Reconstruction of Part of a Book
of New Hall Patterns

No original book recording patterns used by New Hall has been found or recorded. But the association of particular numbers and patterns on New Hall porcelain points strongly to the factory's maintaining a pattern book. Furthermore, the obvious change and development in style of decoration and shape of wares as the pattern numbers get higher indicate that patterns were added to the book in direct sequence.

Although we must not assume that the number of new patterns introduced each year was constant, the figure for an average yearly output is nevertheless useful. With cautious application such a figure has helped to build up and fill in the outline of the productive life of the factory. Pattern number 1830 is the highest one which has been seen added to a piece marked also with the concentric-rings mark. Pattern number 2359 which is on a London-shape milk-jug with the more angular handle is illustrated (Plate 371) and Philip Miller has recorded pattern number 2576 on a London-shape teapot. If the teapot illustrated in Plate 88 was made by New Hall then the pattern book had reached 3639 before the close in 1835.

It is a remarkable coincidence that the pattern book contained about one thousand different patterns when the factory changed from the manufacture of hard-paste to bone-china. This was not contrived, since patterns up to number 1048 have been seen on hard-paste, and the country scenes of pattern number 984 were applied more often to the bone-china body. If the change to bone-china occurred about 1814 (see page 48) then we can estimate that an average of about thirty new patterns a year were introduced during the hard-paste period and between eighty and one hundred and thirty during the bone-china period.

Very few of the early shapes were marked with a pattern number and the large silver-shape and the oval-based waisted teapots had been introduced before the numbers were applied regularly. This suggests that there was no pattern book during the first few years and that one was made only when the proprietors were confident of the success of their venture. It is possible that they were impelled to take this step by requests for repeat orders or for replacement pieces. Perhaps the introduction of a pattern book and the marking of pattern numbers were part of the rationalisation which was marked by the release of Duvivier and the production of only standard services?

Collectors must be very careful not to use the pattern on a piece of porcelain as an indicator of its date of manufacture. Since patterns were often used over a long period of time the only information to be gleaned from this source is a piece's earliest possible date of manufacture. Its shape, and in some cases the nature of the paste and glaze, are the only true guides to its date.

I hope that the format for the pattern book reconstruction will be easily understood. The patterns illustrated on the right-hand page are described on the left-hand page together with some extra patterns. These extra patterns may have been illustrated elsewhere in the book or may be easily recognised as colour variants of illustrated patterns. Whilst I do know of more patterns than have been illustrated, only in a few cases have I described them. I have refrained from mere descriptions of patterns because of the difficulty of translating words into mental images. The descriptions of the patterns given in the following pages are thus intended to be used in conjunction with the illustrations. Frequently only the border and the main decoration are included since only these are common to most of the pieces of a service. The small, supplementary sprigs that complete a pattern usually vary in number and position on different pieces so that generalisation here is impossible.

Interpretation of colour is individual and agreement is rarely possible when words replace the visual image. It is earnestly hoped that the colours recorded here can be recognised.

Pattern 3 *(Plates 7 and 125)*
Border: Two pink bands between which are pink circles with blue dot centres. Main spray: A pink flower out of which grows a mauve flower and a stem of three mauve flowers; the leaves are in two different greens. Second spray: A blue pimpernel out of which grows a pink rose and a yellow bud.

These sprays are known beneath different borders.

Pattern 5 *(Colour Plate F)*
This number has been recorded only under the plate illustrated in Colour Plate F painted by Fidelle Duvivier. It probably refers to the mazarine-blue and gold border, the nature of the scene being irrelevant.

Pattern 12 *(Plate 126)*
All the decoration is in pink enamels.

Pattern 20 *(Colour Plate I, Plates 29 (right), 35, 79 and 80)*
Border: One straight and one arched iron-red line. Alternately, one magenta blob and four blue blobs are attached to the lower line. Main decoration: The figure with the iron-red parasol wears blue, magenta and yellow clothes, and the figure offering a magenta flower wears magenta, blue and yellow clothes.

A sequel to this pattern shows only the person with the parasol who is holding the flower. The magenta and blue blobs in the border are reversed.

Pattern 22 *(Plates 1, 11, 81 and 127)*
Border: Plum-red criss-cross lines and dots between a blue line and a sequence of blue semicircles. Main spray: A plum-red flower with iron-red stamens. The leaves are in two greens.

Pattern 52 *(Plates 29 (left), 31 and 52)*
All the decoration is gold. See also pattern 84.

Pattern 53 *(Plate 53)*
Border: Gold. Overall simple sprigs with a magenta flower and gold leaves.

Pattern 62
All-gold variant of pattern 98 (Plate 36, centre).

Pattern 64 *(Plate 128)*
Gold rim and an inner gold line. There is no other decoration.

Patterns 138, 175, 176 and 283 are related.

Pattern 67 *(Plates 34, 67 and 129)*
Border: Magenta scale band between iron-red lines. Pendent from a pink rose with four green leaves are mauve swags in the centre of which are iron-red pimpernels.

Pattern 78 *(Plates 8 and 13)*
A variant of pattern 67 in which the scale border is broken with a mauve and magenta device.

Pattern 81 *(Plate 130)*
All the decoration is gold.

Pattern 83 *(Colour Plate L)*
All gold except for the rose and foliage insets. The colour of the rose varies between pink and mauve and the foliage can be four simple leaves or delicate tracery and leaves.

125. Pattern 3. Rare fluted CUP with scroll handle.
Height 7 cm (2.75 in), 1782–7.
See page 100.

128. Pattern 64. Clip-handled JUG. Gold pattern number.
Height 10.8 cm (4.25 in), 1782–90. *See page 74.*

126. Pattern 12. Clip-handled TEAPOT with rare flower-shaped knob.
Height 12.7 cm (5 in), 1782–7. *Norfolk Museums Service, Norwich Castle Museum. See page 51.*

129. Pattern 67. Barrel-shaped JUG with corrugated moulding and scroll handle.
Height 7.6 cm (3 in), 1782–5.

127. Pattern 22. Sparrow-beak JUG.
Height 6.4 cm (2.5 in), 1782–7.
See page 71.

130. Pattern 81. STAND for faceted drum-shaped teapot.
Diameter 16 cm (6.3 in), 1782–7.
See Plate 16.

Pattern 84 *(Plate 131)*
Similar to pattern 52 except the straight line is in green and there are green trefoils branching from it on the opposite side to each gold loop.

Pattern 89 *(Colour Plate L)*
Border: Gold chain with a magenta line within each link and two magenta trefoils between each pair of links.

Pattern 90 *(Plate 132)*
Gold rim and undulating line. Magenta pimpernels and purple leaves.

Pattern 94 *(Plate 133)*
Gold rim and inner dentil ring with two black lines between. Within these lines are swags of magenta husks between gold pendants.
    There is a blue variant.

Pattern 98 *(Plate 36, centre)*
Border: Undulating blue dot line intersecting a straight chain of two-tone green husks. A red dot between each husk. The rims are usually brown.
    Pattern 62 is an all-gold variant.

Pattern 121 *(Plates 15 and 134)*
Border: Iron-red bells have a spray of green leaves and pink and mauve florets hanging from them. These bells are linked by a mauve line with a magenta feather at each end. Magenta sprigs are scattered over the body of all pieces.

Pattern 122 *(Plates 14 and 135)*
Border: A chain of magenta hearts between two iron-red lines. Beneath the lower line are a straight and a looped line. Blue dots are within the loops. The other border is a green undulating line which crosses a chain of magenta hearts.

Pattern 133 *(Plate 136)*
All the decoration is black.

131.   Pattern 84. Clip-handled JUG. Height 10.8 cm (4.25 in), 1782–90.

132.   Pattern 90. Faceted SUCRIER with moulded pine-cone knob. Height 14 cm (5.5 in), 1782–90. *See page 82.*

133.   Pattern 94.

135.   Pattern 122.

136.   Pattern 133. STAND for silver-shape
       teapot.
       Length 17.8 cm (7 in), 1790–1805.

134.   Pattern 121. Rare footed JUG with
       corrugated moulding and scroll handle.
       Height 11.4 cm (4.5 in), 1782–5.
       See page 80.

Pattern 136 *(Plate 137)*
All gold except for an orange dot in the centre of the flowers.

Pattern 138
A gold rim. No other decoration.

Patterns 64 (Plate 128), 175, 176 and 283 are related.

Pattern 139 *(Plates 36 (left), 73 and 77)*
Border: Magenta festoons linked by iron-red lines beneath a straight iron-red line. Main spray: A realistic pink rose with a mauve flower behind. Green leaves.

Pattern 140 *(Plate 138)*
Border: Pale-pink wash with a darker-pink pattern of loops and dots painted over. On the outside is an iron-red line and on the inside a yellow-green line overpainted with a black zigzag line. Main spray: Pink rose with a mauve flower behind. Green leaves.

Pattern 141
It is probable that this pattern, described and illustrated in *New Hall and Its Imitators*, was not correctly identified. I do not know where the illustrated bowl is to check the characteristics. On the other hand, many pieces made by another factory using the pattern number 141 have been noted.

Pattern 142 *(Plate 139)*
Border: Curling brown feathers intersecting an undulating line of gold dots. The intersection is marked by large dots in gold. All other rims and bands are plain gold.

Pattern 144 *(Plate 140)*
Border: A line of mauve dots below a single iron-red line and above a double iron-red line. Beneath this is an undulating line of green leaves and coloured flowers. Main spray: Back-to-back pink and mauve flowers. Green leaves.

Pattern 145 *(Plate 141)*
Decoration is all gold except for the underglaze dark-blue flower outlined with gold at the bottom of each swag.

Pattern 245 is similar.

Pattern 148 *(Plate 142)*
Decoration is all gold except for the feathers in the intertwining border and part of the knot of the wreaths which are orange.

Pattern 152 *(Plate 17)*
Underglaze mazarine-blue pattern completed with overglaze gold decoration.

Pattern 153 *(Colour Plate J)*
Underglaze mazarine-blue completed with overglaze gold decoration.

Pattern 154 *(Plate 51)*
The zig-zag lines are in underglaze mazarine-blue, all the other decoration is overglaze gold.

137.   Pattern 136.

138.   Pattern 140.

139. Pattern 142.

141. Pattern 145. STAND for faceted
drum-shaped teapot.
Diameter 16.3 cm (6.4 in), 1782–7. *See
Plate 16.*

142. Pattern 148.

140. Pattern 144. Clip-handled JUG.
Height 8.8 cm (3.5 in), 1782–90.

Pattern 155 *(Plate 143)*
Underglaze mazarine-blue band completed with overglaze gold decoration.

Pattern 156 *(Plate 144)*
Underglaze mazarine-blue scrolls completed with overglaze gold decoration.

Pattern 157 *(Plate 145)*
Border: Iron-red. Main decoration: The two outside figures are dressed in magenta, blue and yellow clothes but the central figure wears magenta trousers. The table is in iron-red. The foreground and leaves are in two shades of green.

The same main decoration was also used with a border of blue semicircles.

Pattern 161 *(Plate 146)*
Border: Green leaves on mauve stems with blue and red buds between two gold lines. The sprigs on the body of the pieces are alternately gold and coloured.

Pattern 166 *(Plate 147)*
All of the festoon is gold. The single florets are in a soft green.

Pattern 167 *(Plates 37 and 148)*
Border: A narrow apricot-peach coloured band between two gold lines set below the gold rim of the piece. The body of the piece is decorated with gold sprigs which are larger than those of pattern 206 (Plate 3).

Pattern 254 is a colour variant.

143.   Pattern 155. Reeded obconical JUG.
Height 10.2 cm (4 in), 1787–93.
See page 74.

144.   Pattern 156. Reeded PLATE. Enamelled pattern number.
Diameter 20.1 cm (7.9 in), 1787–93.

145.   Pattern 157.

147.   Pattern 166.

146.   Pattern 161.

148.   Pattern 167. TEACUP with rarely found
'Spode' handle.
Height 5.7 cm (2.25 in). *City Museum and
Art Gallery, Stoke-on-Trent. See page 89.*

Pattern 168 *(Plate 149)*
Very pale-apricot festoons hang from the border used in pattern 167 (Plate 148).

Pattern 170 *(Plate 50)*
Underglaze mazarine-blue scrolls completed with overglaze gold decoration.

Pattern 171 *(Plate 150)*
The 'basket' pattern. Borders: Mauve dots between two iron-red lines. An undulating dotted and continuous brown line. Main spray: A brown basket filled with coloured flowers with green leaves.

This pattern was used by other factories using pattern numbers 16 (Turner) and 112.

Pattern 172 *(Plate 151)*
The 'mauve ribbon' pattern. Border: Undulating mauve ribbon crossed by a magenta straight line. Beneath the mauve loops are magenta bristles and above the loops are alternately a sprig of a pink and mauve rose and a sprig of two iron-red buds. The body of the piece is scattered with coloured sprigs.

This pattern was used by other factories using pattern numbers 113, 117 and 129.

Pattern 173 *(Plate 152)*
Borders: Pink scale edged with two thin brown lines. Coloured sprays hang from this border; alternate ones contain a mauve rose-bud. An undulating continuous and dotted brown line. The body of the piece is scattered with coloured sprigs.

Pattern 175
A gold rim and small gold single sprigs.
Patterns 64 (Plate 128), 138, 176 and 283 are related.

Pattern 176
No rim decoration. Only small gold sprigs on the body.
Patterns 64 (Plate 128), 138, 175 and 283 are related.

Pattern 180 *(Plate 153)*
The rim and stars are gold.

149.   Pattern 168.

150.   Pattern 171. Helmet-shaped JUG with squashed-in body. This smaller size has a clip handle.
Height 8.8 cm (3.5 in), 1782–93. *See Plate 37 and page 74.*

151. Pattern 172. Reeded helmet-shaped JUG with loop handle.
Height 8.8 cm (3.5 in), 1782–93.
See page 74.

152. Pattern 173. Quatrefoil SPOON-TRAY.
Length 14 cm (5.5 in), 1782–7.
See page 95.

153. Pattern 180. COVERED SUCRIER with moulded pine-cone knob and JUG, both with spiral fluting. Gold pattern numbers.
Sucrier height 14 cm (5.5 in), 1787–90. *Godden Collection. See pages 74, 82.*

Pattern 181 *(Plate 154)*

Border: Pale-green band with everything else gold.

Pattern 182 *(Plate 155)*

The dots are of sea-green or turquoise enamel, all other decoration is gold.

Pattern 183 *(Plate 156)*

Border: Pink roses within gold ovals set in a band composed of green dots within mauve dotted ovals. All other decoration is gold.

Pattern 186 *(Plate 157)*

The 'red ribbon' pattern. Borders: Red undulating ribbon with coloured sprigs within the loops. Undulating green-leaf line with occasional pink and mauve roses crossing two thin iron-red lines. Some junctions feature an iron-red star-like device. Most pieces have coloured sprigs scattered over the body.

This pattern was used by other factories using pattern numbers 116 and 126.

Pattern 188 *(Plate 158)*

The rim, two straight lines and the dotted undulating line are gold. The other undulating line has green leaves on it and pairs of orange hips.

Pattern 191 *(Plate 159)*

Border: Undulating green-leaf line crossing two thin straight black lines. Magenta pimpernels appear at the intersections. Main spray: Coloured pimpernel-like flowers and green leaves.

154.   Pattern 181. Obconical JUG. Enamelled pattern number.
       Height 11.7 cm (4.6 in), 1787–93.

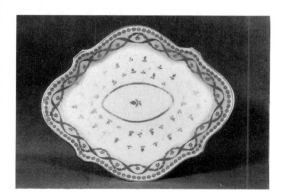

155.   Pattern 182. STAND for silver-shape teapot.
       Length 17.8 cm (7 in), 1787–1805.

156.   Pattern 183.

158.   Pattern 188.

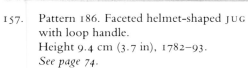

157.   Pattern 186. Faceted helmet-shaped JUG
with loop handle.
Height 9.4 cm (3.7 in), 1782–93.
See page 74.

159.   Pattern 191. Reeded obconical JUG.
Height 11.4 cm (4.5 in), 1787–93.

Pattern 195 *(Plates 30 and 160)*

Border: A complex border which features iron-red string-like and magenta festoons. Main spray: A pink and a mauve rose, green leaves, two sprays of iron-red florets and a single pink rose.

This pattern was used by other factories using the pattern numbers 2 (Turner), 7 (Minton), 124, 125, 145 and 189 (Herculaneum).

Pattern 196 *(Plate 161)*

The decoration is gold except for the ferns which are blue and magenta.

Pattern 198 *(Plate 19)*

All the decoration is gold.

Pattern 202 *(Plate 162)*

Border: Dark-blue underglaze blobs with two magenta enamel petals behind. The rest of the decoration is gold.

Pattern 206 *(Plate 3)*

A broad yellow band between two gold lines. The upper of these two lines is the rim of the piece (when a bowl or cup or saucer). The body of the piece is decorated with small gold sprigs.

Patterns 223 (Plate 166), 227, 244 and 283 are other colour variants.

Pattern 208 *(Plate 163)*

Border: Undulating line of orange dots intersecting a continuous straight line of blue arrowheads beneath a black line. Main spray: A green broad leaf separating two pink roses. Iron-red and mauve florets and green leaves complete the spray.

Pattern 213 *(Plate 82)*

The florets of the spray are mainly pale-blue with a few magenta lines added. The rest of the decoration is gold.

Pattern 216 *(Plate 164)*

Gold rim and line. Brown band with white diamonds and ovals. Magenta swags.

Pattern 221

Yellow colour variant of pattern 222 (Plate 165).

Pattern 222 *(Plate 165)*

Border: A broad apricot-peach band with a gold and a black line above and a black line with a

160.   Pattern 195. MUG.
Height 12.2 cm (4.8 in), 1787–1800.
See page 96.

161.   Pattern 196.

gold, small leaf-and-berry edging below. The whole is set below the gold rim of the piece.

Pattern 221 is a yellow colour variant.

162. Pattern 202.

164. Pattern 216. PLATE. Enamelled pattern number.
Diameter 21.3 cm (8.4 in).

163. Pattern 208. Silver-shape JUG of small size. Enamelled pattern number.
Height 9 cm (3.6 in), 1787–95.
See page 74.

165. Pattern 222. Silver-shape JUG with spiral fluting. Note the two vertical columns and compare it with the jug in Plate 235. Enamelled pattern number.
Height 10.7 cm (4.2 in), 1790–5.
See page 74.

Pattern 223 *(Plate 166)*
Pink colour variant of pattern 206 (Plate 3).
Patterns 227, 244 and 283 are other colour variants.

Pattern 227
Apricot-peach colour variant of pattern 206 (Plate 3).
Patterns 223 (Plate 166), 244 and 283 are other colour variants.

Pattern 230 *(Plate 167)*
Border: Underglaze mazarine-blue band with gold. Sprays of underglaze blue and gold.

Pattern 238 *(Plate 168)*
Border: The medallions are coloured with peach-apricot enamel and there are magenta trefoils. The rest of the decoration is gold.

Pattern 240 *(Plate 169)*
Underglaze mazarine-blue with overglaze gold decoration.

Pattern 241 *(Plate 83)*
Border: Undulating red dotted line crossing another undulating line which features leaves and florets. Alternate crests show a pink rose and a pink pimpernel. Main spray: Back-to-back pink and mauve roses are the main feature. The upper green leaves are usually vigorously lance-like and the bottom pair of leaves are usually arranged almost horizontally and are iron-red in colour.
The same pattern number was used when the decoration was used in black only.
This pattern was used by other factories using the pattern numbers 2 (Miles Mason), 136 and 218. Also by the Caughley-Coalport factory.

Pattern 243 *(Plate 40)*
Underglaze mazarine-blue completed with overglaze gold decoration.

Pattern 244
Royal-blue colour variant of pattern 206 (Plate 3).
Patterns 223 (Plate 166), 227 and 283 are other colour variants.

Pattern 245
Some pieces have been noted with this number and a pattern which is very similar to pattern 145 (Plate 141) except that the shapes of the underglaze blue flowers are slightly different.

Pattern 248 *(Plate 54)*
Underglaze mazarine-blue completed with overglaze gold decoration.

Pattern 251 *(Plate 170)*
Underglaze mazarine-blue completed with overglaze gold decoration.

Pattern 253 *(Plate 74)*
Borders: Mauve ornamental line below a thin iron-red line. Undulating plain iron-red and dotted mauve lines. Main spray: Back-to-back mauve and pink flowers with a flat-headed mauve flower and two green leaves growing out from them. Three iron-red leaves are featured beneath.
This decoration is also found in black and the same pattern number is used.

Pattern 254
A mole-coloured variant of pattern 167 (Plate 148).

Pattern 257 *(Plate 171)*
A narrow black band between two gold lines. The upper of these is the rim. Beneath the lower line is a zig-zag line in gold. On plates and some saucers there is a similar inner narrow band of decoration. The body is decorated with small gold sprigs.
Pattern 258 is a pale-pink colour variant.

Pattern 258
A pale-pink colour variant of pattern 257 (Plate 171).

Pattern 259 *(Plate 172)*
Border: There are either blue or red dots within the spaces in the gold lattice. All other decoration is gold.

Pattern 264
An all-gold variant of pattern 288 (Plate 180).

166.   Pattern 223.

169.   Pattern 240.

167.   Pattern 230.

170.   Pattern 251.

171.   Pattern 257.

168.   Pattern 238.

172.   Pattern 259.

Pattern 266 *(Plate 173)*
Border: Most of this is gold. The more ornate festoons bear red berries and have a red quatrefoil at the bottom of the loop. The rest of the decoration is gold.

Pattern 267 *(Plates 119 (centre) and 174)*
Border: A thin iron-red line from which hangs a mauve undulating line. Main spray: Green leaves, a pink rose and a number of small coloured florets.

The same pattern number was used when the decoration was in black only.

Pattern 270 *(Plate 175)*
All the decoration is gold.

Pattern 271
An all-gold variant of pattern 275 (Plate 61), the parallelogram areas between the gold ones being uncoloured.

Pattern 272
Border: Narrow, often smudged, underglaze pale-blue transfer-print. The overall pattern is an underglaze blue transfer-print with some of the leaves and flowers coloured with orange, magenta and green enamels on top of the glaze.

Patterns 274, 360, 490 (Colour Plate N) and 856 (Plate 305) use the same transfer-printed outline pattern.

Pattern 273 *(Plate 176)*
Border: Magenta scale between a thick magenta and a thin iron-red line. Below this latter is a mauve looped line from which hang small

magenta buds and three small green leaves. Main spray: The centre is a pink rose, behind which is half of a deep-mauve flower. There are green leaves and a small pink rose as well as iron-red florets.

Pattern 274
This pattern is the same as pattern 272 to which has been added a considerable amount of gold. This is mostly to outline the border and the many leaves in the pattern.

Patterns 360, 490 (Colour Plate N) and 856 (Plate 305) use the same transfer-printed outline pattern.

Pattern 275 *(Plate 61)*
The decoration is almost all gold. The groups of three parallelograms are coral coloured.

Pattern 271 is an all-gold variant.

Pattern 280 *(Plate 177)*
Border: An undulating black line to which are attached black and gold trefoils and gold and magenta dots.

Pattern 282 *(Plate 178)*
All the decoration is gold.

Pattern 283
An all-gold pattern. Gold rim and gold band below with no colour between. Small gold sprigs on the body. It is best described as pattern 206 (Plate 3) without the yellow.

Patterns 64 (Plate 128), 138, 175 and 176 are also very simple all-gold patterns.

173. Pattern 266.

176. Pattern 273.

174. Pattern 267.

177. Pattern 280.

175. Pattern 270. TEAPOT LID from an 'old oval shape' teapot.

178. Pattern 282.

Pattern 285 *(Plates 122 (left) and 179)*
The strawberries and leaves are in two tones of sepia, the rest is gold.

Pattern 288 *(Plate 180)*
Border: Gold design and lines. Magenta or orange dots are attached to the undulating gold line. The sprigs, which are usually scattered on the body of the pieces, are magenta (or orange) and gold. The centres of saucers usually feature an attractive magenta (or orange) foxglove-like flower with gold leaves.

Pattern 264 is an all-gold variant.

Pattern 289 *(Plate 181)*
Border: Orange-brown band within two gold lines. The rest of the decoration is gold.

Patterns 301, 306 and 307 are other colour variants.

Pattern 290 *(Plate 182)*
All gold except for the florets, which are mauve.

Pattern 291 *(Plate 183)*
All gold except for large orange dots and groups of three berries, each of which has some added black decoration.

Pattern 294
Black variant of pattern 295 (Plate 184).

Pattern 295 *(Plate 184)*
All painted in orange (or sometimes iron-red) enamel.

Pattern 294 is a black variant.

179.   Pattern 285.

180.   Pattern 288.

181. Pattern 289.

183. Pattern 291.

182. Pattern 290.

184. Pattern 295. Silver-shape JUG. Enamelled pattern number.
Height 10.8 cm (4.25 in), 1790–1805.

Pattern 296 *(Plate 185)*
Border: An iron-red line below which is a sea-green band between black lines, below which is a magenta line with fine hairs. Main spray: Pink and mauve flowers, magenta pimpernels and green leaves.

Pattern 297 *(Colour Plate M)*
Border: An interrupted orange band from which is scratched a zig-zag line between two black lines. The interruptions are mauve stems leading to a pink floret and three pairs of green leaves. Main spray: A mauve multi-petalled flower with an iron-red centre, a pink flower and a spray of four iron-red florets with green leaves in two shades.
    Pattern 298 (Plate 186) is a border variant.

Pattern 298 *(Plate 186)*
The same main spray as pattern 297. Border: A thin iron-red line and a thin mauve line to which is attached by pink flower buds an undulating mauve line. There are blue dots beneath the pink flower buds.
    Pattern 297 (Colour Plate M) is a border variant.

Pattern 300 *(Plate 187)*
Gold except for occasional magenta flowers in the border and in the body sprig.

Pattern 301
All-gold variant of patterns 289 (Plate 181), 306 and 307, i.e. there is no colour and the gold design starts at the rim.

Pattern 303 *(Plate 188)*
All the decoration is gold.

Pattern 306
Mazarine-blue variant of patterns 289 (Plate 181), 301 and 307.

Pattern 307
Pink variant of patterns 289 (Plate 181), 301 and 306.

Pattern 308 *(Plate 69)*
All black enamel.
    Pattern 328 is a coloured variant.

Pattern 311 *(Plate 189)*
Border: Three iron-red lines. Between the outer two is a row of pink arrowheads and groups of three dots. Between the inner two is pink scale interrupted by vignettes painted in black. The larger ones contain two iron-red rose buds on the black foliage. The remainder of the piece is covered with scattered sprigs. The central sprig has only one pink rose. The leaves are painted in two shades of green.

Pattern 312 *(Plate 190)*
Border: Iron-red line beneath which is a feathery mauve line joining deep-pink flowers with four pairs of leaves. Main spray: A deep-pink rose and three puce-coloured pansy-like flowers amidst leaves of two shades of green. A pink flower bursting from its green bud climbs upwards from the group.

185.   Pattern 296. Silver-shape JUG. Enamelled pattern number.
Height 10.8 cm (4.25 in), 1790–1805.

186.   Pattern 298. PLATE with spiral fluting. Enamelled pattern number.
Diameter 20.6 cm (8.1 in), c. 1795.

187. Pattern 300.

189. Pattern 311.

188. Pattern 303.

190. Pattern 312. Obconical JUG. Enamelled
pattern number.
Height 11.4 cm (4.5 in), 1787–97.

Pattern 314 *(Plate 191)*

Orange flowers and buds, the rest is gold.

Pattern 316 *(Plate 192)*

Orange-brown enamel fills the semicircles which are outlined and overpainted with black. The rest of the decoration is gold except for the arcs of dots and groups of three dots which are black.

Pattern 317 *(Plate 193)*

Border: Between gold lines, the upper of which is on the rim of the piece, are light-purple leaves and alternate gold and iron-red flowers.

A similar pattern was used by Minton as pattern 79 and Miles Mason as pattern 422.

Pattern 318 *(Plate 194)*

Pink flowers and buds, the rest is gold.

Pattern 319 *(Plate 195)*

Border: The central panel contains two bunches of grapes and the florets in the adjacent panels are blue. The rest of the decoration is gold.

Pattern 324 *(Plate 196)*

The flower heads on the sprays are sepia, the rest is gold.

Pattern 326

The decoration is a narrow gold border around the piece.

Pattern 328 *(Plate 20)*

A polychrome variant of pattern 308 (Plate 69). The border is magenta and orange-brown. The basket and ribbon are orange-brown and all leaves of the flowers and sprigs are green.

191.   Pattern 314. Silver-shape JUG. Enamelled pattern number.
Height 10.8 cm (4.25 in), 1790–1805.

192.   Pattern 316.

193.   Pattern 317.

195.   Pattern 319.

194.   Pattern 318.

196.   Pattern 324.

Pattern 329 *(Plate 197)*
The oak leaves and the acorn cups are sepia, the rest is gold.

Pattern 330 *(Plate 198)*
The flower heads are pale magenta, the rest is gold.

Pattern 336 *(Plate 199)*
All the decoration is in blue enamel on the glaze.

Pattern 338 *(Plate 39)*
Border: Mauve undulating line interrupted by sprays containing a pink rose. Main spray: A wheel painted with black, pink, orange, pink, etc. sectors within a wreath of pink roses, orange pimpernels and leaves painted in two shades of green.

Pattern 339 *(Plate 201)*
Border: The florets in the foliage are mainly blue with magenta lines added. All the rest is gold except for some of the dots on the lower undulating line which are magenta.

Pattern 342 *(Plate 200)*
Border: Underglaze blue transfer-print. Main spray usually consists of pink and mauve flowers with green leaves. The rim is sometimes gold.

Pattern 343 *(Plate 202)*
Underglaze mazarine-blue band with overglaze gold decoration.

Pattern 344
Black variant of pattern 546 (Plate 71) and 547.

197. Pattern 329. Silver-shape J U G. Enamelled pattern number.
Height 10.7 cm (4.2 in), 1790–1805.

198. Pattern 330.

201.   Pattern 339.

199.   Pattern 336. COFFEE-POT. Enamelled
pattern number.
Height 25.4 cm (10 in), 1787–1810.

202.   Pattern 343.

200.   Pattern 342. PLATE. Enamelled pattern
number.
Diameter 20.4 cm (8 in).

Pattern 346 *(Plate 203)*
Magenta hips, the rest is gold.

Pattern 347 *(Plate 204)*
The ground inside the circles is dark-brown, the rest is gold.

Pattern 348 *(Plate 205)*
The leaves and hips are dark-brown, the rest is gold.

Pattern 351 *(Plate 206)*
The circles are dark-mauve, the rest is gold.

Pattern 353 *(Plates 43 and 207)*
Border: The outer border, which is inside a tea-bowl, is mauve-magenta beneath a thin black line. Lower down is a chain of mauve and green. Main spray: Pink and mauve flowers with two shades of green-coloured leaves.

Pattern 354 *(Plate 208)*
Border: Red scale patches outlined with thin black lines and beneath a thin black line. A continuous line of arrowheads. Main spray: Pink and mauve back-to-back roses are the main feature.

A silver-shape teapot in the Victoria and Albert Museum is decorated with this pattern and the words 'Sophia Sayer 1803'.

Pattern 360
A colour variant of patterns 272, 274, 490 (Colour Plate N) and 856 (Plate 305).

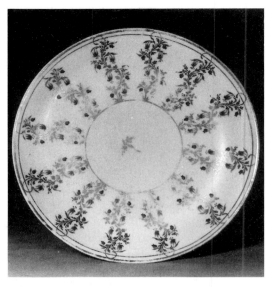

203.   Pattern 346. PLATE. Enamelled pattern number.
Diameter 20.6 cm (8.1 in).

204.   Pattern 347.

205.   Pattern 348. BOWL. Enamelled pattern number.
Diameter 15.5 cm (6.1 in).

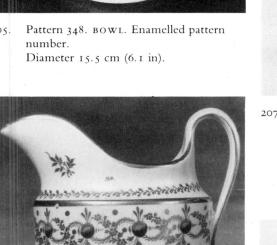

207.   Pattern 353. Faceted obconical JUG. Enamelled pattern number. Height 10.2 cm (4 in), 1787–93. *City Museum and Art Gallery, Stoke-on-Trent. See page 74.*

206.   Pattern 351. JUG which accompanied the 'old oval shape' teapot. Enamelled pattern number.
Height 11.4 cm (4.5 in), 1795–1805.

208.   Pattern 354. *City Museum and Art Gallery, Stoke-on-Trent*

Pattern 362 *(Plate 209)*

The decoration is mostly gold. The large triangles and the daisy heads are magenta and there are some magenta florets on the gold tracery.

Pattern 363

A mauve variant of pattern 365 (Plate 210).

Pattern 365 *(Plate 210)*

The flowers are orange-red, the rest is gold.

   Pattern 363 is a mauve colour variant.

Pattern 366 *(Plate 211)*

Border: Mostly iron-red. The sprigs on the border contain pink, mauve and iron-red florets and green leaves. Main spray: Rather insignificant florets tied with iron-red string.

Pattern 367 *(Plate 212)*

Black monochrome enamel.

   Patterns 598 and 599 are colour variants.

Pattern 369 *(Plate 213)*

The semicircles on alternate sides of the line going round the piece are magenta, the rest is gold.

Pattern 373 *(Plate 214)*

Pattern 373 consists of the main decoration depicted in Plate 214 with a single orange-brown line inside the rim; it has no other border. The pattern number of the border variant illustrated is not known. On bowls the decoration rambles round in *famille rose* style. On saucers and plates the patterns can be seen to be in two parts. The left-hand of the sprays has two pink flowers, a small orange one and then a medium-sized orange one with three blue leaves below it. The other spray has a large double flower and a small orange and blue flower. The leaves are green.

209.   Pattern 362.

210.   Pattern 365.

211. Pattern 366.

213. Pattern 369.

212. Pattern 367.

214. Pattern 373.

Pattern 376 *(Plate 215)*

The sprays in the main border and the main spray of the pattern feature a pink rose and two yellow-centred flowers amongst green leaves and florets coloured blue and blue with yellow centres. Mauve sprigs are scattered over the rest of the piece.

Pattern 377 *(Plate 216)*

Main spray: The star-shaped flower is magenta with blue and then yellow within. The buds are light-brown with black dotted outline and the leaves are green with black marks painted on them.

Pattern 379

Variant of pattern 382 (Plate 217) in which the band is in brown instead of green.

Pattern 382 *(Plate 217)*

Black rim. Green band between two black lines and with black overdecoration. The zig-zag below is in black and orange.

Pattern 379 is a colour variant.

Pattern 398 *(Plate 218)*

Border: The framework is gold and the background of some sections is coral-pink. The flowers in the large frame are a bright magenta-red.

A similar pattern is often referred to as the 'Church Gresley' pattern.

Pattern 408 *(Plate 219)*

Underglaze mazarine-blue band, the rest is gold.

Pattern 415 *(Plate 220)*

Blue rim. Black festoons; one set of these has yellow and green enamel decoration added.

This pattern was used by Pinxton and by Minton (pattern number 18).

Pattern 420

All-black variant of pattern 430 (Plate 227) and 515.

This pattern was also used by Minton (pattern number 44).

215.   Pattern 376. Silver-shape JUG. Enamelled pattern number.
Height 10.8 cm (4.25 in), 1790–1805.

216.   Pattern 377. Silver-shape JUG. Enamelled pattern number.
Height 10.8 cm (4.25 in), 1790–1805.

217. Pattern 382. BOWL. Enamelled pattern number.
Diameter 15.2 cm (6 in).

219. Pattern 408.

220. Pattern 415.

218. Pattern 398.

Pattern 421 *(Plate 221)*

Border: Iron-red. Foreground and background are black and iron-red. The boy has a magenta top and green trousers, the middle figure is all blue, the right-hand figure has a green gown on top of a red skirt.

Pattern 431 depicts the same group of people wearing different coloured clothes.

Pattern 422 *(Plate 222)*

All the pattern is painted with blue and pink enamels. Most of the flowers are blue and the leaves and stems are pink. The rim band is blue or gold.

Pattern 423

A thick gold rim with a thin gold line within. The central decoration is a bat-print in black of a spray of flowers.

Pattern 425 *(Plates 88 (left) and 223)*

The 'window' pattern.

Plate 224 shows a bone-china dessert-plate numbered 425. The scene on this plate is often found inside punch-bowls decorated on the outside with the 'window' pattern.

Pattern 1066 is a bone-china version with a slightly different border.

Pattern 426 *(Plates 56 and 225)*

Gold rim band and thin inner line. The main spray consists of well-painted flowers. Different pieces in a service may have different flowers in the spray. Additional sprigs are in gold.

Pattern 427 *(Plate 226)*

Underglaze mazarine-blue band with overglaze gold decoration.

221.   Pattern 421.

222.   Pattern 422.

223.   Pattern 425. QUART MUG. Enamelled
pattern number.
Height 12.7 cm (5 in), 1795–1800.
See page 96.

225.   Pattern 426. SUCRIER. This shape usually
accompanied the small boat-shaped
teapot.
Height 11.5 cm (4.5 in), 1795–1805.
See page 85.

224.   Pattern 425. DESSERT-PLATE. Enamelled
pattern number.
Diameter 19.6 cm (7.7 in), bone-china,
1815–25. *See page 93.*

226.   Pattern 427. SUCRIER with applied spiral
fluting. Such fluting was not often applied
to this shape. Plate 245 shows the shape
of jug which would be *en suite*. Enamelled
pattern number.
Height 13.2 cm (5.2 in), 1795–1805.
See Plate 56 and page 85.

Pattern 430 *(Plate 227)*
Gold rim. Dark-brown wheatears.
   Patterns 420 and 515 are different-coloured variants.

Pattern 431
Colour variant of pattern 421 (Plate 221). The middle figure has a magenta top and a yellow skirt and the right-hand figure has a green gown on top of a blue underskirt. The pattern and the rest of the colours are the same as pattern 421.

Pattern 433
Black monochrome variant of pattern 467 (Plate 241).

Pattern 434 *(Plate 228)*
Brown or gold rim. Iron-red tendrils and stems have blue flowers and light-green leaves on them.
   Pattern 747 is a black monochrome variant.

Pattern 435
See pattern 436.

Pattern 436 *(Plate 229)*
The jug illustrated, and other pieces in the service were marked 436. The vignettes were in dark-sepia; the vertical dividing lines and the inside lines of the diamonds were mauve; the rest was gold. Some pieces have been seen with orange-coloured vignettes and some with blue enamel in place of the mauve. Some sets have been numbered 435 but there seems to be no consistent relationship between the numbers and the colours.

Pattern 437 *(Plate 230)*
The undulating line is mauve. All other decoration is gold.

Pattern 439 *(Plate 231)*
The narrow band is orange-brown, the rest is gold.

Pattern 441 *(Plate 232)*
The rim, inner thin line and undulating stem with foliage are gold. Clusters of black leaves and pairs of orange berries are attached to the stem.

Pattern 442 *(Plate 233)*
Border: Magenta inside and thin iron-red outside. Border sprays have a principal orange flower, green leaves and two ferns in dotted iron-red. Simple coloured sprigs around the body.

Pattern 443
This pattern is very similar to pattern 521. The main differences seem to be in the number of groups of leaves which hang from the rim of a piece and the number and size of the streamers of berries.

227.   Pattern 430. STAND for oval convex-sided teapot. Enamelled pattern number. Length 17.1 cm (6.75 in), 1795–1805. *See Plate 22.*

228.   Pattern 434. *City Museum and Art Gallery, Stoke-on-Trent.*

231. Pattern 439.

232. Pattern 441.

229. Pattern 436. JUG which accompanied an 'old oval shape' teapot. Enamelled pattern number.
Height 11.4 cm (4.5 in), 1795–1805.

230. Pattern 437. PLATE. Enamelled pattern number.
Diameter 20.8 cm (8.2 in).

233. Pattern 442. Silver-shape JUG. Enamelled pattern number.
Height 10.7 cm (4.2 in), 1790–1805. *City Museum and Art Gallery, Stoke-on-Trent.*

Pattern 445 *(Plate 234)*
The fuchsia-like flowers are underglaze blue with pink enamel lines around the edges. The rest of the decoration is gold.

Pattern 446 *(Plate 58)*
The tree and its base leaves are in underglaze blue and outlined with gold. The berries are orange. Other leaves are formed with grey stems and red dots and outlined with gold dots.

Pattern 449 *(Plates 38 and 235)*
Border: Chains of pimpernels and leaves between large orange-brown blobs. Main spray: Pink and mauve back-to-back flowers are in the centre of the spray, which is within a magenta line frame.

Pattern 450 *(Plate 236)*
Border: Undulating purple line crossing with an undulating chain of leaves and small flowers. Main spray: Back-to-back pink and mauve flowers are at the centre.

Pattern 451 *(Plate 237)*
The grapes are mauve, the leaves are green, the rest is gold.

Pattern 455 *(Plate 238)*
Orange monochrome decoration.

Pattern 459
Broad orange-brown band with all other decoration in gold.
   Pattern 554 (Plate 257) is a mazarine-blue colour variant.

234.   Pattern 445.

235.   Pattern 449. Silver-shape JUG with spiral-fluting going all round the jug (compare with Plate 165). Enamelled pattern number.
Height 10.7 cm (4.2 in), 1790–1805.
See page 74.

236. Pattern 450. Silver-shape TEAPOT. Enamelled pattern number.
Height 15.2 cm (6 in), 1790–1805. *City Museum and Art Gallery, Stoke-on-Trent.*

237. Pattern 451.   238. Pattern 455.

Pattern 461 *(Plate 239)*

Black monochrome decoration.

Pattern 462

Rim and thin inner line in gold. The main decorations are black bat-prints.

Patterns 466 (Plate 240), 511 (Plate 248), 709 (Plate 283) and 1063 (Plate 108) use the same prints but have different borders.

Pattern 465

This number has been seen only on pieces decorated with underglaze blue transfer-prints with added gilding and probably refers to the added gold decoration.

Pattern 466 *(Plate 240)*

Rim and undulating leafed line in gold. The main decorations are black bat-prints.

Patterns 462, 511 (Plate 248), 709 (Plate 283) and 1063 (Plate 108) use the same prints but have different borders.

Pattern 467 *(Plate 241)*

Borders: Top border is an iron-red band over-drawn with black lines. Lower border is iron-red lines and ribbon with coloured florets and leaves in alternate loops. Main spray: The colours used are darker than usually painted being mostly magenta and purple. Two shades of green are used for the leaves.

Pattern 433 is a black monochrome variant.

Pattern 471 *(Plate 242)*

Border: The blossoms are painted in pale-blue with red tendrils. The rest of the pattern is gold.

Pattern 472 *(Plate 243)*

Gold rim. The left-hand end of each panel is washed in with mauve enamel and the rest of the decoration is black enamel.

Pattern 473

This number has been seen only on pieces decorated with underglaze blue transfer-prints with added gilding and probably refers to the added gold decoration.

Pattern 478 *(Plate 244)*

The berries are mauve and black and the rest of the decoration is gold.

Pattern 586 is an orange-coloured variant.

239.   Pattern 461. STAND for small-sized boat-shaped teapot. Enamelled pattern number.
Length 16.5 cm (6.5 in), 1795–1805. *City Museum and Art Gallery, Stoke-on-Trent. See Plate 23.*

240.   Pattern 466. JUG which accompanied 'old oval shape' teapot. Enamelled pattern number.
Height 11.4 cm (4.5 in), 1795–1805. *See Colour Plate N.*

241. Pattern 467.

243. Pattern 472.

242. Pattern 471.

244. Pattern 478.

Pattern 480 *(Plate 245)*
All the decoration is gold.

Pattern 484 *(Plate 42)*
The tree trunks, leaves and nuts are in underglaze mazarine-blue and orange. The rest of the decoration and the rim are gold.

Pattern 487
Blue bat-print variant of pattern 559 (Plate 21).

Pattern 490 *(Colour Plate N)*
Border: Underglaze mazarine-blue between gold lines and with gold leaf-and-berry motif. The pattern utilises the same underglaze transfer outline design as patterns 272, 274, 360 and 856 (Plate 305). Some of the leaves are coloured with underglaze mazarine-blue and others with orange, magenta or green.

Pattern 499 *(Plate 246)*
Underglaze mazarine-blue band. Red centre dot to the flowers. The rest of the decoration is gold.

There is an orange-coloured variant of this pattern.

Pattern 504
An all-gold variant of pattern 505 (Plate 247).

Pattern 505 *(Plate 247)*
Underglaze mazarine-blue band. The rest of the decoration is gold.

Pattern 511 *(Plate 248)*
Black bat-prints with gold rim and a more complex arabesque gold band than is used for pattern 466 (Plate 240).

Patterns 462, 466, 709 (Plate 283) and 1063 (Plate 108) use the same prints but have different gold borders.

Pattern 515
Blue-coloured variant of patterns 420 and 430 (Plate 227).

Pattern 520 *(Plate 249)*
A Chinese courtyard-scene painted in coloured enamels.
N.B. This pattern was erroneously given the number 530 in *New Hall and Its Imitators*.

Pattern 521 *(Plate 250)*
The grey leaves are overpainted with fine orange dots and the berries are orange. The rest of the decoration is gold.

This pattern is very similar to pattern 443 and was used by Minton (pattern 85).

245.   Pattern 480. JUG with applied spiral
        fluting *(see Plate 226)*. Enamelled pattern
        number.
        Height 11.4 cm (4.5 in), 1795–1805.
        *See page 74. City Museum and Art Gallery,
        Stoke-on-Trent.*

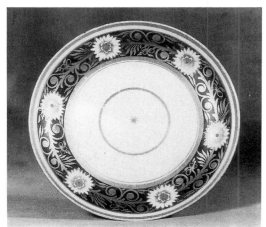

246.   Pattern 499.

247. Pattern 505. SUCRIER which would
accompany the small boat-shaped teapot.
Enamelled pattern number.
Height 11.4 cm (4.5 in), 1795–1805.
See page 62.

249. Pattern 520.

248. Pattern 511.

250. Pattern 521. Large boat-shaped JUG.
Enamelled pattern number.
Height 8.4 cm (3.3 in), 1800–10.
See page 78.

Pattern 524 *(Plate 251)*
Underglaze mazarine-blue leaves and acorn husks. The rest of the decoration is gold.

Pattern 533 *(Plate 252)*
Underglaze mazarine-blue band. Green and yellow bunches of grapes. The rest of the decoration is in gold

Pattern 538 *(Plate 253)*
Underglaze mazarine-blue with the rest of the decoration in gold.

Pattern 540 *(Plate 70)*
Underglaze mazarine-blue background and outline to the flowers and leaves in the pattern. The decoration is completed with gold.

Pattern 541 *(Plate 254)*
Border: Magenta scale areas from a black line band. Main spray: Tall iron-red vase with a spray of flowers and leaves. Two magenta-coloured flowers, one above the other, are the main feature.

Pattern 542 *(Plate 255)*
All-gold decoration.

Pattern 545 *(Plate 256)*
Gold rim and inner thin line between which is the decoration in two tones of brown.

Pattern 546 *(Plate 71)*
Gold rim and small sprigs. The roses are orange.
　　Patterns 344 and 547 are colour variants.

Pattern 547
Pieces coloured both in sepia and in light-brown have been noted. The different colours may be due to the firing.
　　Pattern 344 and 546 (Plate 71) are colour variants.

Pattern 550 *(Plate 55)*
The animal and trees are in underglaze mazarine-blue and decorated with gold lines and dots. The animal has a red mouth and there are some red dots in the background.

Pattern 551
Mazarine-blue colour variant of pattern 651 (Plate 277).

251.　　Pattern 524.

252.　　Pattern 533.

253. Pattern 538.

255. Pattern 542.

254. Pattern 541.

256. Pattern 545. PLATE. Enamelled pattern number.
Diameter 20.6 cm (8.1 in).

Pattern 554 *(Plate 257)*
Mazarine-blue colour variant of pattern 459.

Pattern 556 *(Plate 62)*
Very broad underglaze mazarine-blue band. The rest of the decoration is gold.

Pattern 557 *(Plate 258)*
The two large 'roses' are purple, the groups of three 'roses' are pale-pink. The leaves are in orange and in different shades of green. The rim and some leaf veins are gold.

Pattern 558
Orange colour variant of pattern 695 (Plate 282).

Pattern 559 *(Plate 21)*
The bat-print is in black. The rest of the decoration is gold. Cups and saucers have different scenes from the teapot.
   Pattern 487 is a blue colour variant.

Pattern 562 *(Plate 259)*
The leaves, acorns and flowers are in underglaze mazarine-blue. The rest of the decoration is in gold.

Pattern 563 *(Plate 260)*
Underglaze mazarine-blue and gold.

Pattern 566 *(Plate 261)*
Underglaze mazarine-blue and gold.

Pattern 568 *(Plate 262)*
The fronds and ferns between the two gold lines are partly gold and partly iron-red.

Pattern 570
See pattern 752 for the description and comment.

257.   Pattern 554.

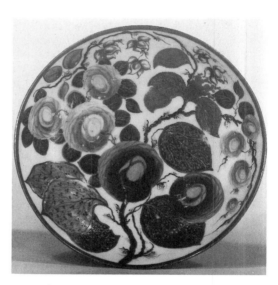

258.   Pattern 557.

259. Pattern 562.

261. Pattern 566.

260. Pattern 563.

262. Pattern 568.

Pattern 571 *(Plate 263)*
Underglaze mazarine–blue and gold. The flowers are in coloured enamels.

Pattern 572 *(Plate 288)*
See pattern 752 for the description and comment.

Pattern 575 *(Plate 264)*
Underglaze mazarine–blue and gold.
  An orange-coloured variant was made.

Pattern 581 *(Plate 265)*
Underglaze mazarine–blue and gold.

Pattern 583 *(Plate 266)*
Underglaze mazarine–blue and gold.

Pattern 585 *(Plate 267)*
Underglaze mazarine–blue and gold.

Pattern 586
An orange berry variant of pattern 478 (Plate 244).

Pattern 593 *(Plate 22)*
Border: Pale-blue hatching with magenta devices in the insets. Main spray: The main flower and the two florets to its left are pink. Attached to these flowers are blue florets or leaves (five). Climbing out of the spray at the top is a small pansy in mauve and yellow. The leaves are in two shades of green.

Pattern 594 *(Plate 268)*
Border: Iron-red. Main spray: The very rambling spray features flowers in orange and yellow. The leaves are in two shades of green.

263.   Pattern 571.

264.   Pattern 575. BOWL. Enamelled pattern number.
Diameter 15.5 cm (6.1 in).

265.   Pattern 581.

267.   Pattern 585.

266.   Pattern 583. SUCRIER which would
       accompany the small boat-shaped teapot.
       Enamelled pattern number.
       Height 11.4 cm (4.5 in), 1795–1805.
       See page 62.

268.   Pattern 594. Silver-shape JUG. Enamelled
       pattern number.
       Height 10.8 cm (4.25 in), 1790–1805. *City
       Museum and Art Gallery, Stoke-on-Trent.*

Pattern 596 *(Plate 269)*

Border: Iron-red line with a magenta line beneath. From this latter hang swags of green and magenta dots and arrowheads. Main spray: Magenta flower with iron-red centre and a broad green leaf. Other leaves in two shades of green.

Pattern 598

Orange-coloured variant of pattern 367 (Plate 212) and 599.

Pattern 599

Borders: Orange undulating dotted line with alternate blue and magenta florets hanging in alternate loops. The other chain is orange. Main spray: Large magenta rose and leaves in two shades of green.

Patterns 367 (Plate 212) and 598 are monochrome colour variants.

Pattern 603 *(Plate 23)*

Border: Pairs of broad brown leaves are linked by green leaf-and-floret loops and pendants. Small pink roses are on the ends of the pendants. Main spray: The two flowers are brown and magenta. The leaves are in two shades of green.

Pattern 604

This number has been seen only on pieces decorated with underglaze blue transfer-prints with added gilding and probably refers to the added gold decoration.

Pattern 605 *(Plate 41)*

Pink border overpainted with magenta. The largest spray is a single pink rose with green leaves.

Pattern 611 *(Plate 270)*

Borders: Gold rim. Underglaze mazarine-blue band between gold lines. Gold chain. Main decoration: Underglaze mazarine-blue and gold basket filled with realistically painted flowers in coloured enamels.

Pattern 621 *(Plate 271)*

Oriental scene sometimes referred to as 'dinner is served'.

Pattern 673 is similar.

Pattern 623 *(Plate 272)*

Underglaze mazarine-blue and gold.

Pattern 630 *(Plate 273)*

Underglaze mazarine-blue and gold.

Pattern 631 *(Plate 274)*

Underglaze mazarine-blue and gold.

269.   Pattern 596.

270.   Pattern 611. STAND for large boat-shaped teapot. Enamelled pattern number. Length 16.5 cm (6.5 in), 1800–10. *Godden Collection. See Plate 310.*

271. Pattern 621. PLATE. Enamelled pattern
number.
Diameter 22.8 cm (9 in). *See page 96.*

273. Pattern 630. Large boat-shaped JUG.
Enamelled pattern number.
Height 8.6 cm (3.4 in), 1800–10.
See page 78.

272. Pattern 623.

274. Pattern 631. Large boat-shaped JUG.
Enamelled pattern number.
Height 8.6 cm (3.4 in), 1800–10.
See page 78.

Pattern 636 *(Plate 275)*
Underglaze mazarine-blue and gold.

Pattern 638 *(Plate 276)*
Underglaze mazarine-blue and gold.

Pattern 651 *(Plate 277)*
Orange band, the rest of the decoration is gold.
　Pattern 551 is a mazarine-blue colour variant.

Pattern 653 *(Plate 278)*
Underglaze mazarine-blue and gold.

Pattern 660
Variant of pattern 748 (Plate 24) with blue funnel-like devices.

Pattern 662 *(Plate 279)*
Border: Interrupted orange band from which is scratched a zig-zag line and on which are painted blue dots. Blue dots and angled lines are attached to the orange scalloped line. Main spray: This features a magenta rose and a flower with five purple petals and a yellow centre.

Pattern 670
Orange colour variant of pattern 692 (Plate 281).

Pattern 673
A variant of pattern 621 (Plate 271) in which the picture is surrounded by mainly gold decoration.

Pattern 686 *(Plate 280)*
Border: Magenta scale band between two iron-red lines. Main spray: Puce and magenta back-to-back flowers.

275.　Pattern 636.

276.　Pattern 638.

277. Pattern 651.

279. Pattern 662.

278. Pattern 653.

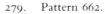

280. Pattern 686. Silver-shape JUG. Enamelled pattern number.
Height 10.8 cm (4.25 in), 1790–1805. *City Museum and Art Gallery, Stoke-on-Trent.*

Pattern 692 *(Plate 281)*

Underglaze mazarine-blue and gold. Sometimes the broad band is just below the rim and with a gold band below it.

Pattern 670 is a colour variant.

Pattern 695 *(Plate 282)*

Underglaze mazarine-blue and gold.

Pattern 558 is an orange colour variant.

Pattern 709 *(Plates 44 and 283)*

Black rim. A variety of black bat-prints is used, some of them being of named places.

Patterns 462, 466 (Plate 240), 511 (Plate 248) and 1063 (Plate 108) use the same prints but have different border decoration. See also patterns 984, 1053 and 1159 (Plate 330).

Pattern 736 *(Plate 284)*

Underglaze mazarine-blue and gold.

Pattern 737 *(Plate 285)*

Underglaze mazarine-blue leaves, orange berries and the rest of the decoration is gold.

Pattern 746 *(Plate 286)*

Border: Magenta arrowheads and dots in sequence between two thin black lines. Magenta scale decoration fills in between simple enamel flower sprays. Main spray: Orange-brown basket and a blue ribbon. Main flower is magenta.

Pattern 791 (Plate 298) uses the same border but has a different spray.

Pattern 747

Black monochrome variant of pattern 434 (Plate 228).

Pattern 748 *(Plate 24)*

Border: Orange and brown funnel-like devices are linked with leaf-and-floret chains. Main spray: Single magenta rose and green leaves in two shades.

Pattern 660 is a colour variant.

281.   Pattern 692.

282.   Pattern 695.

283.   Pattern 709. JUG which would
accompany the 'new oval shape' teapot
(Plate 24). Enamelled pattern number.
Height 9.1 cm (3.6 in), c. 1810.
See page 78.

285.   Pattern 737.

286.   Pattern 746.

284.   Pattern 736.

Pattern 752 *(Plates 84 and 287)*

The foreground, house and trees are in underglaze mazarine-blue with some pale-blue. The pattern is completed with orange and gold. Teapots, sucriers and jugs do not have a border. Bowls, cups, saucers and plates have a gold border as well as the gold rim. The pattern number depends upon this border. The muffin-dish shown in Plate 84 bears the mark 752 and was part of a service numbered 570. The borders for both patterns were simple gold undulating leafy lines with occasional orange dots. There were only slight differences between 570 and 752. On the other hand, pattern 572 (Plate 288) has a border with gold bell-like buds pointing in the same direction and with two orange dots between.

Pattern 753 *(Plate 289)*

Gold rim and thin line. The printed decoration is in black.

Pattern 761 *(Plate 290)*

Underglaze mazarine-blue background with some small pale-blue blobs completed with gold.

Pattern 763 *(Plate 291)*

Orange background, pink strawberries and green centres to the leaves. The rims and other decoration are gold.

Pattern 770 *(Plate 292)*

Orange ground with green leaves. The rest of the decoration is gold.

Pattern 775 *(Plate 293)*

The narrow bands are in underglaze mazarine-blue. The pairs of leaves of the meander are bright-blue. The rest is gold.

287.   Pattern 752. Part of a MUFFIN-DISH (Plate 84). Enamelled pattern number.

288.   Pattern 572.

289.   Pattern 753. PLATE. Enamelled pattern number.
Diameter 20.9 cm (8.25 in).

290.   Pattern 761.

292.   Pattern 770. STAND for large boat-shaped
        teapot. Enamelled pattern number.
        Length 17.1 cm (6.75 in), 1800–10.
        See Plate 310.

291.   Pattern 763.

293.   Pattern 775.

Pattern 777 *(Plate 294)*
Underglaze mazarine-blue background. The flower devices have orange and some light-blue added. The rest of the decoration is gold.

Pattern 779 *(Plate 295)*
Underglaze mazarine-blue ground. The grapes are green and yellow. The rest of the decoration is gold.

Pattern 783 *(Plate 296)*
Iron-red monochrome decoration.

Pattern 789 *(Plate 297)*
Chinese courtyard-scene in coloured enamels. The rim and much of the border are gold.

Pattern 791 *(Plate 298)*
The same border as pattern 746 (Plate 286). Instead of the basket of flowers there is a simple red rose and green leaves.

Pattern 799 *(Plate 299)*
Border: Single pink roses between iron-red scrolls. The main spray consists mainly of a pink rose and green leaves.

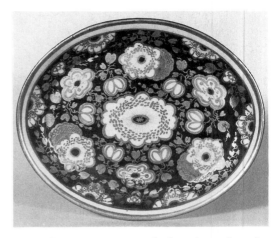

294.   Pattern 777. STAND for large boat-shaped teapot. Enamelled pattern number. Length 17.1 cm (6.75 in), 1800–10. *See Plate 310.*

295.   Pattern 779. COVERED CHOCOLATE-CUP. Enamelled pattern number. Height 10.8 cm (4.25 in), 1795–1800. *See page 101.*

296. Pattern 783. SUGAR-BASIN. Enamelled
pattern number.
Diameter 12 cm (4.75 in).

298. Pattern 791.

299. Pattern 799. Small boat-shaped TEAPOT.
Enamelled pattern number.
Height 13.7 cm (5.4 in), 1795–1805.

297. Pattern 789.

Pattern 812 *(Plate 300)*
Underglaze mazarine-blue broad band with orange flowers. The white leaves are alternately groups of three and two. The rest of the decoration is gold.

Pattern 827 *(Plate 301)*
Underglaze mazarine-blue framework. The orange trefoils have black lines on them. The rest of the decoration is gold.

Pattern 829 *(Plate 302)*
Underglaze mazarine-blue leaves. Orange strawberries. The rest of the decoration is gold.

Pattern 835 *(Plate 303)*
Underglaze mazarine-blue and gold.

Pattern 839 *(Plate 304)*
Border: Thin iron-red line. Undulating green leafed line with attached magenta florets alternating with pairs of blue dotted florets. There is no main spray.

Pattern 846 *(Plate 307, right)*
The main decoration is an on-glaze bat-print in gold using Warburton's patented process and the same engraved plates as were used for patterns 462, 466 (Plate 240), 511 (Plate 248) and 709 (Plate 283). The underglaze mazarine-blue border is over-decorated with gold. This gold pattern determines the pattern number.

Pattern 888 (Plate 307, left) uses a different gold decoration.

Pattern 856 *(Plate 305)*
The same outline transfer-print as was used for pattern 272 was used for this pattern. Underglaze mazarine-blue is used as an overall background and much of the pattern is left unpainted. The leaves which are painted are treated with orange and green. The whole of the decoration is completed with gold.

Patterns 272, 274, 360 and 490 (Colour Plate N) used the same transfer-printed outline pattern.

300.   Pattern 812.

301.   Pattern 827. SUCRIER which would accompany the large boat-shaped teapot. Enamelled pattern number.
Height 13.3 cm (5.25 in), 1800–10.

302. Pattern 829. Large boat-shaped JUG.
Enamelled pattern number.
Height 8.6 cm (3.4 in), 1800–10.
See page 78.

304. Pattern 839. Silver-shape JUG. Enamelled
pattern number.
Height 10.8 cm (4.25 in), 1790–1805.

303. Pattern 835.

305. Pattern 856.

Pattern 880 *(Plate 306)*
Underglaze mazarine-blue and gold.

Pattern 888 *(Plate 307, left)*
The gold design on top of the mazarine-blue ground establishes the pattern number. Pattern 846 (Plate 307, right) uses a different gold decoration.

Pattern 901 *(Plate 308)*
The florets have five underglaze blue, five overglaze orange and five gold petals. The rest of the decoration is gold.

Pattern 911 *(Plate 309)*
Blue rim. Alternate red, blue and green sprigs and black ferns.

Pattern 914 *(Plate 310)*
Large realistic roses and green leaves. The rest of the decoration is gold.

Pattern 921 *(Plate 311)*
Underglaze mazarine-blue band. The white flowers have orange seeds. The leaves are green. The rest of the decoration is gold.

Pattern 924 *(Plate 57)*
Underglaze mazarine-blue and gold.

307.   *Left*, pattern 888; *right*, pattern 846. The gold decoration determines the pattern number.

308.   Pattern 901.

306.   Pattern 880.

309.   Pattern 911.

310. Pattern 914. Large boat-shaped TEAPOT. Enamelled pattern number.
Height 15.2 cm (6 in), 1800–10. *City Museum and Art Gallery, Stoke-on-Trent.*

311. Pattern 921. Large boat-shaped JUG. Enamelled pattern number.
Height 8.3 cm (3.25 in), 1800–10.

Pattern 934 *(Plate 312)*
Narrow sea-green band between gold lines. Black on-glaze print of a basket of flowers.

Pattern 940 *(Plate 313)*
Blue rim. The rambling spray features a large blue flower which has eight petals with an iron-red inner line. The three florets to the right of this flower have yellow centres. The flower on the left features five yellow dots with black outlines. These are attached to another blue and iron-red petalled head.

Pattern 947 *(Plate 314)*
Border: Pink band overpainted with pink lines and dots and interrupted by yellow moths outlined in black. This band is between iron-red lines. Main spray: large yellow flower surrounded by green and iron-red leaves and tendrils.

Pattern 953 (Plate 315)
Border: Iron-red rim and line. Magenta roses and knots. Mauve dotted loops and feathers. Main spray: Single magenta rose and green leaves in two shades.

Pattern 984 *(Plate 72)*
The bat-prints used for pattern 709 (Plate 283) etc. overpainted with coloured enamels. Gold rim on cups and cans; an inner gold line is added on saucers and plates.

Patterns 1053, 1092 and 1159 (Plate 330) are border or background variants.

Pattern 1033 *(Plate 316)*
Blue rim and pink border band. Sepia coloured bat-prints.

Pattern 1040 *(Plate 25)*
Coloured enamels.

Pattern 1043 *(Plate 317)*
The florets are blue and orange. The rest of the decoration is gold.

312.   Pattern 934.

313.   Pattern 940. BOWL. Enamelled pattern number.
Diameter 20.6 cm (8.1 in).

314. Pattern 947.

316. Pattern 1033.

315. Pattern 953.

317. Pattern 1043. Large boat-shaped JUG.
Enamelled pattern number.
Height 8.2 cm (3.25 in), 1800–10.

Pattern 1045 *(Plate 318)*
Yellow rim. Inner border: Iron-red circles connected by green lines. Iron-red dots. The centre decoration features a yellow shell. The orange-red trefoils have black centre marks.

A similar pattern was used by several other factories, numbers 29 and 811 are known.

Pattern 1046 *(Plate 319)*
The decoration is mainly gold with additions in iron-red enamel.

Pattern 1053
The same coloured bat-prints as pattern 984 enclosed within concentric gold-and-black circles.

Patterns 1092 and 1159 (Plate 330) are border or background variants.

Pattern 1054 *(Plate 320)*
Most of the decoration is underglaze dark- and light-blue. The rest is gold.

See also pattern 1214.

Pattern 1057 *(Plate 321)*
Underglaze mazarine-blue frame and leaves with some of the flowers in iron-red. The rest of the decoration is gold.

Pattern 1058 *(Plate 322)*
Gold rim. The roses are pink-red, the leaves are blue- and yellow-green.

Pattern 1059 *(Plate 27)*
Underglaze mazarine-blue and gold.

Pattern 1063 *(Plate 108)*
Black bat-prints; mostly classical scenes but some are rural scenes. Black rim and inner line.

Probably a bone-china extension of pattern 709 (Plate 283) which was used on hard-paste (cf. pattern 1100).

Pattern 1064 *(Plate 323)*
The flowers from left to right are in pink, yellow and brown enamels. The tendrils and the rim are in blue.

Pattern 1066
The 'window' pattern, number 425 (Plate 223), with a different border for use on bone-china.

318. Pattern 1045. Miniature flanged PLATE. Concentric-rings mark and enamelled pattern number. Diameter 11.2 cm (4.4 in), bone-china, 1815–20.

319. Pattern 1046. PLATE. Enamelled pattern number.
Diameter 19.1 cm (7.5 in), hard-paste. *City Museum and Art Gallery, Stoke-on-Trent.*

320.   Pattern 1054. PLATE. Enamelled pattern
number.
Diameter 21.6 cm (8.5 in), bone-china.

322.   Pattern 1058. SAUCER. Concentric-rings
mark, bone-china. *City Museum and Art
Gallery, Stoke-on-Trent.*

321.   Pattern 1057. London-shape JUG.
Enamelled pattern number.
Height 8.2 cm (3.25 in), bone-china,
1815–25.

323.   Pattern 1064. London-shape JUG.
Enamelled pattern number.
Height 8.2 cm (3.25 in), bone-china,
1815–25.

Pattern 1084 *(Plates 32 and 324)*
Yellow rim and blue inner line with iron-red and blue decoration between. The main decoration is in orange and blue enamels. There is no green.

This pattern was used by other factories using numbers 20 (Machin), 222 and 488 (Copeland and Garrett).

Pattern 1085 *(Plate 325)*
Underglaze mazarine-blue is used for the border, stems and some leaves and petals. The remainder is orange, pale-blue and green.

Pattern 1092
The same coloured bat-prints as are used for pattern 984 within an underglaze powder-blue band overdecorated with gold. Coloured bat-prints of fruit are in circular reserves.

Patterns 984, 1053 and 1159 (Plate 330) use the same coloured bat-prints.

Pattern 1100
Grey-black bat-prints used in pattern 709 (Plate 283) with gold rim and, on saucers and plates, an inner gold rim. Perhaps a bone-china number for pattern 462 which was used on hard-paste?

Pattern 1109
Black bat-prints of 'mother and child' subjects after Adam Buck (see page 118). Rim and inner line are black.

Patterns 1147 (Plates 26 and 328), 1178, 1236, 1277 (Colour Plate Q) and 1525 (Plate 354) use these prints also.

Pattern 1126 *(Plate 326)*
Pale-blue ground between two mazarine-blue bands with gold overdecoration. The flowers are pink and orange. Between them are two pairs of white leaves, outlined in gold and on gold stems, and a pair of green leaves.

Pattern 1141 *(Plate 327)*
All the decoration is gold.

Pattern 1147 *(Plates 26 and 328)*
Allegorical and 'mother and child' bat-prints in black within gold borders.

Patterns 1109, 1178, 1236, 1277 (Colour Plate Q) and 1525 (Plate 354) use the 'mother and child' prints.

Pattern 1153 *(Plate 329)*
Underglaze mazarine-blue foreground and tree with orange flowers and green leaves. Rim and tree outlined in gold.

324.   Pattern 1084. COVERED BOWL with entwined-twig handles and knob. Enamelled pattern number. Height 12.7 cm (5 in), 1815–30. *See pages 101, 103.*

325.   Pattern 1085.

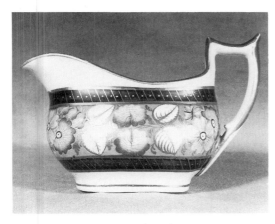

326. Pattern 1126. London-shape JUG.
Enamelled pattern number.
Height 8.6 cm (3.4 in), 1820–30.

328. Pattern 1147. STAND for transitional
teapot (Plate 26). Enamelled pattern
number.
Length 17.5 cm (6.9 in), 1810–15.
See page 67.

327. Pattern 1141.

329. Pattern 1153.

Pattern 1159 *(Plate 330)*

The same coloured bat-prints as are used for pattern 984 within an underglaze mazarine-blue band overdecorated with gold. Coloured bat-prints of fruit are in the reserves.

Patterns 984, 1053 and 1092 use the same coloured bat-prints.

Pattern 1161 *(Plate 331)*

Underglaze mazarine-blue leaves, stems and acorns. The flower centres are orange. The rest of the decoration is gold.

Pattern 1163 *(Plate 332)*

Mainly underglaze mazarine-blue with some pale-blue and orange decoration. The rest of the decoration is gold.

Pattern 1172 *(Plate 333)*

Oriental design in coloured enamels.

Pattern 1178

Similar to pattern 1147 but with a less ornate border.

Patterns 1109, 1147 (Plates 26 and 328), 1236, 1277 (Colour Plate Q) and 1525 (Plate 354) use the same prints.

Pattern 1180 *(Plate 334)*

Bright-pink between blue lines and below blue rim. The coloured flower spray features a pink rose and green leaves.

Pattern 1214

This is a similar design to pattern 1054 (Plate 320) with a pouncing lion in place of the elephant.

Pattern 1218 *(Plate 335)*

Two underglaze mazarine-blue bands outlined and overpainted with gold. Between them on a pale-blue ground are alternate pink and orange flowers with green leaves.

330.   Pattern 1159. SAUCER. *City Museum and Art Gallery, Stoke-on-Trent.*

331.   Pattern 1161. London-shape JUG. Enamelled pattern number. Height 8.4 cm (3.3 in), 1815–25. *City Museum and Art Gallery, Stoke-on-Trent.*

332.   Pattern 1163.

334.   Pattern 1180. London-shape JUG.
Concentric-rings mark and enamelled
pattern number.
Height 8.4 cm (3.3 in), 1815-25.

333.   Pattern 1172. PLATE. Enamelled pattern
number.
Diameter 20.4 cm (8 in). *City Museum and
Art Gallery, Stoke-on-Trent.*

335.   Pattern 1218.

Pattern 1235 *(Plate 336)*
Black or brown rim. Green leaves. The large flowers, stems and outlined sprays are in orange.

Pattern 1236
The bat-prints of 'mother and child' scenes used for pattern 1109 are overpainted with coloured enamels. Gold rim and inner line added.

Patterns 1147 (Plates 26 and 328), 1178, 1277 (Colour Plate Q) and 1525 (Plate 354) use the same coloured prints.

Pattern 1267 *(Plate 337)*
Underglaze mazarine-blue and gold decoration.

Pattern 1277 *(Colour Plate Q and Plate 63)*
The same coloured bat-prints as are used for pattern 1236 are set within an underglaze mazarine-blue ground. There are vignettes of coloured bat-prints of fruit. The whole decoration is completed with gold.

Patterns 1147 (Plates 26 and 328), 1178, 1236 and 1525 (Plate 354) use the same coloured bat-prints.

Pattern 1296 *(Plate 338)*
Blue rim. Brown border from which hang swags with green leaves and a pink rose.

Pattern 1304 *(Plate 339)*
Two underglaze mazarine-blue bands outlined and decorated with gold. On a pale-blue ground between them are large pink-edged flowers, clusters of orange flowers and green leaves.

Pattern 1313 *(Plate 59)*
Underglaze mazarine-blue foreground, tree and branches. The flowers are mainly pale-pink and the leaves are green.

Pattern 1318 *(Plate 340)*
Pale-blue ground between a gold line and a mazarine-blue band overpainted in gold. Large pale-pink flowers with gold and magenta centres. The tendrils and leaves are in gold.

Pattern 1357 *(Plate 341)*
Gold rim and coloured bat-print of fruit.

336.   Pattern 1235.

337.   Pattern 1267. PLATE. Enamelled pattern number.
Diameter 20.4 cm (8 in).

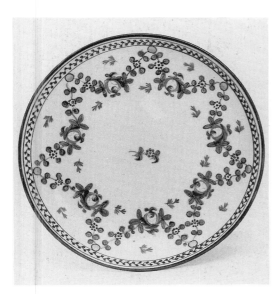

338. Pattern 1296. PLATE. Concentric-rings mark and enamelled pattern number. Diameter 19.3 cm (7.6 in). *City Museum and Art Gallery, Stoke-on-Trent.*

340. Pattern 1318. London-shape JUG. Enamelled pattern number. Height 8.4 cm (3.3 in), 1815–25.

339. Pattern 1304. STAND for London-shape teapot. Enamelled pattern number. Length 19.1 cm (7.5 in), 1815–30.

341. Pattern 1357.

Pattern 1373 *(Plate 342)*

Underglaze mazarine-blue border, tree stem and leaves. Pale-blue ground. There are some orange-brown flowers and one with yellow petals and a magenta centre. The rest of the decoration is gold.

Pattern 1397 *(Plate 343)*

Gold rim. The bunches of flowers are an outline transfer-print overpainted with coloured enamels.

This pattern was illustrated in Colour Plate H in *New Hall and Its Imitators*.

Pattern 1401 *(Plate 344)*

Between the two gold lines the repeated flowers in pink and yellow are connected by magenta stems with green leaves and some small blue flowers.

Pattern 1403 *(Plate 45)*

The rim and border lines are gold. The flowers are pink and the leaves green.

Pattern 1415 *(Plate 345)*

Underglaze mazarine-blue border to a pale-blue ground. Orange strawberries with green leaves. The rim, border decoration, tendrils and leaf outline are in gold.

Pattern 1435 *(Plate 346)*

Brown rim, brown tree trunk and rock. From the trunk are iron-red florets and green leaves. From the rock the flowers are in yellow, mauve and blue.

Pattern 1442 *(Plate 347)*

Yellow-orange enamel rim. The main spray features a mauve flower with a yellow centre and a smaller yellow flower.

Pattern 1444 has a blue rim.

Pattern 1444

The decoration is the same as that of pattern 1442 (Plate 347). The rim is blue instead of yellow-orange.

342.   Pattern 1373. STAND for London-shape teapot. Enamelled pattern number. Length 19.1 cm (7.5 in), 1815–30. *City Museum and Art Gallery, Stoke-on-Trent.*

343.   Pattern 1397. Demi-tasse CUP. Height 5.7 cm (2.25 in). *City Museum and Art Gallery, Stoke-on-Trent.*

344. Pattern 1401.

346. Pattern 1435.

345. Pattern 1415.

347. Pattern 1442. PLATE. Concentric-rings mark and enamelled pattern number. Diameter 21.6 cm (8.5 in). *City Museum and Art Gallery, Stoke-on-Trent.*

Pattern 1458 *(Plate 348)*
Underglaze mazarine-blue border to a pale-blue ground. Large pink flowers with outer petals in shades of mauve. Green leaves. The rim, border decoration, tendrils and some leaves are in gold.

Pattern 1474 *(Plate 349)*
Underglaze mazarine-blue ground. The flowers are pink. All other decoration is gold.

Pattern 1477 *(Plate 350)*
Underglaze pale-blue ground to the flange and the major part of the centre. The three sectors are white florets on an orange ground. Pink flowers and gold tendrils and leaf edges on the pale-blue. The inner mazarine-blue band is between gold lines and overdecorated with gold.

Pattern 1478 *(Colour Plate S and Plate 85)*
Underglaze pale-blue ground to the moulded border. Bat-print of fruit, overpainted in colour, in a basket painted in underglaze mazarine-blue and gold. Baskets of flowers and sprays of flowers have also been recorded as decoration but since there was no pattern number on the plates it is not certain whether they really belong to pattern 1478.

Pattern 1480 *(Colour Plate S)*
The background to the moulding and the plate is pink. The flowers are overpainted bat-prints. The rest of the decoration is gold.

Pattern 1485 *(Plate 351)*
The rim and lower lines are gold. The flower is pink and the leaves are green.

Pattern 1496 *(Plate 352)*
Gold rim. From the orange and blue fan sprout (right to left) two purple flowers, three orange buds, an orange-petalled yellow-centred flower and an orange flower. All the leaves are green.

Pattern 1506 *(Colour Plate S)*
Dark-green ground colour all over. Polychrome flowers. Gold rim and added decoration.

Pattern 1511 *(Plate 353)*
Yellow-orange rim. The branch is in brown with a green and then a brown leaf on either side of a magenta flower. The bird has a mauve tail.

348.   Pattern 1458. STAND for London-shape teapot. Enamelled pattern number. Length 19.1 cm (7.5 in), 1815–30.

349.   Pattern 1474. PLATE. Concentric-rings mark and enamelled pattern number. Diameter 19.1 cm (7.5 in). *Godden Collection*.

352.   Pattern 1496. PLATE. Concentric-rings
mark and enamelled pattern number.
Diameter 20.4 cm (8 in).

350.   Pattern 1477. DESSERT-PLATE. Enamelled
pattern number.
Diameter 20.4 cm (8 in).

351.   Pattern 1485. Demi-tasse CUP.
Height 5.7 cm (2.25 in). *City Museum and
Art Gallery, Stoke-on-Trent.*
See Plate 64 and page 92.

353.   Pattern 1511.

Pattern 1525 *(Plate 354)*

The same coloured bat-prints of a 'mother and child' as are used for pattern 1236. The gold line is just below the rim.

Patterns 1147 (Plates 26 and 328), 1178, 1236 and 1277 (Colour Plate Q) use the same coloured bat-prints.

Pattern 1542

Underglaze mazarine-blue stems and leaves outlined with gold. Orange-brown flowers with green leaves. Occasional magenta flowers with yellow centres. The rest of the decoration is gold.

This pattern, not shown here, was illustrated in *New Hall and Its Imitators* (Plate 175).

Pattern 1547 *(Plate 355)*

Blue and red florets amongst green leaves.

Pattern 1560 *(Plate 356)*

Magenta rim line. Complex overglaze printed flower spray coloured with enamels.

Pattern 1563 *(Plate 357)*

The rim and all the decoration is gold except for an orange centre to the main flower of the larger sprays.

Pattern 1597 *(Plate 358)*

Gold rim. There are pink roses and flower heads with magenta fronds. The leaves are green.

Pattern 1614 *(Plate 359)*

Iron-red border. Brown tree and foreground with pink flowers and green leaves. The birds are coloured blue, iron-red and yellow.

Pattern 1623 *(Plate 64)*

Orange-yellow rim. The decoration is in purple enamel.

Pattern 1669

Floral sprays in a green monochrome enamel.

354.   Pattern 1525. COVERED CHOCOLATE-CUP. Enamelled pattern number. Height 15.2 cm (6 in). *City Museum and Art Gallery, Stoke-on-Trent.* *See pages 101, 103.*

355.   Pattern 1547. London-shape JUG. Concentric-rings mark and enamelled pattern number. Height 8.3 cm (3.25 in), 1815–25. *City Museum and Art Gallery, Stoke-on-Trent.*

356. Pattern 1560. London-shape JUG.
Concentric-rings mark and enamelled
pattern number.
Height 8.3 cm (3.25 in), 1815–25.

358. Pattern 1597. PLATE. Enamelled pattern
number.
Diameter 20.4 cm (8 in).

357. Pattern 1563. SAUCER. Concentric-rings
mark.

359. Pattern 1614. PLATE. Concentric-rings
mark and enamelled pattern number.
Diameter 20.4 cm (8 in).

Pattern 1680 *(Plate 360)*

Border: Underglaze mazarine-blue blobs connected by overglaze gold leaves and tendrils. Pattern: Leaves in underglaze mazarine-blue outlined with gold and connected by gold tendrils. The main flower has three large magenta-pink petals, a yellow centre and purple berry-like dots.

Pattern 1681 *(Plate 361)*

Border: Underglaze mazarine-blue band between gold lines and with applied gold decoration. Pattern: The ground and tree are in underglaze mazarine-blue outlined with gold. The branches have orange-brown florets completed with gold. Both birds have magenta and yellow breasts, dark-blue wings and orange tail feathers.

Pattern 1696 *(Plate 46)*

Putty-coloured band between gold lines on which is a continuous string of pink roses, gold leaves and orange buds.

Pattern 1699 *(Plate 362)*

Gold rim and border lines. Continuous string of pink roses with an orange and a blue flower between. Green leaves.

Pattern 1700 *(Plate 363)*

Gold rim and border edges. Open pink flower with black dots. Yellow flower with brown fronds from it. The leaves are green.

Pattern 1706

Pale-blue ground to the rim which has a white moulded tracery design which includes birds (similar to that used for pattern 1707). An inner underglaze mazarine-blue band between gold lines and overdecorated with gold. The central decoration consists of a bat-print of fruit overpainted with coloured enamels and completed with gold.

Pattern 1707 *(Plate 86)*

Pale-blue ground all over. Two underglaze mazarine-blue bands which are normally between gold lines and overdecorated with gold (on the illustrated example the gold is largely rubbed away). Pink roses and green leaves.

Pattern 1831 *(Plate 364)*

The flowers in the meander are mainly pink and blue. The leaves are green.

Pattern 1865 *(Colour Plate R)*

Two underglaze mazarine-blue bands with added gold. Pink roses, green leaves and gold stems and small leaves.

Pattern 1874 *(Plate 365)*

Underglaze pale-blue ground on the flange and two underglaze mazarine-blue bands decorated with gold. Pink roses with green leaves. Gold tendrils and leaves.

360.   Pattern 1680. London-shape TEAPOT. Enamelled pattern number. Height 15.2 cm (6 in), 1815–25. *City Museum and Art Gallery, Stoke-on-Trent.*

361.   Pattern 1681.

362.   Pattern 1699.

364.   Pattern 1831. STAND for London-shape
        teapot. Enamelled pattern number.
        Length 19.1 cm (7.5 in), 1815–30.

363.   Pattern 1700. London-shape JUG.
        Enamelled pattern number.
        Height 8.3 cm (3.25 in), 1815–25.

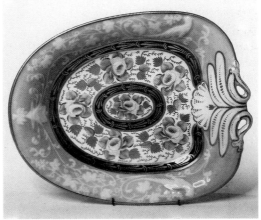

365.   Pattern 1874. DESSERT-DISH. Enamelled
        pattern number.
        Length 19.7 cm (7.75 in), 1820–30.
        Godden Collection.

Pattern 1897 *(Plate 366)*

All the roses are pink with green leaves. Other flowers in various bright enamels with green and yellow leaves.

Pattern 1915 *(Plate 65)*

Gold rim and inner line. Pink roses within green leaves. Groups of five yellow strawberry-like buds.

Pattern 1934 *(Plate 367)*

Hand-painted scenes in coloured enamels. The rest is gold.

Pattern 1944 *(Plate 368)*

Underglaze mazarine-blue band with added gold decoration. The divisions of the moulding are often picked out with gold. The different sprays in the cartouches are in coloured enamels.

Pattern 2050 *(Plate 66)*

The upper and the lower sections of the moulding are green, the two side sections are blue. The flowers are painted in bright enamels. The rings, the cartouche and the sections of the moulding are outlined in gold.

Pattern 2082 *(Plate 28)*

Gold rim. The flowers in the cartouches are bat-printed outlines with added coloured enamels.

Pattern 2103

Gold rim. Wicker-moulding as used for patterns

1944 (Plate 368), 2050 (Plate 66) and 2082 (Plate 28). The only decoration is a pink rose with some green and some gold leaves within the cartouches.

Pattern 2155 *(Plate 369)*

Underglaze blue band. Flower spray in coloured enamels. Other decoration including the over-painting of the raised dot border is gold.

Pattern 2229 *(Plate 87)*

Underglaze pale-blue ground to the four different white relief-moulded sprays. Painted scenes in enamels. Added gold decoration.

Pattern 2240 *(Plate 370)*

Underglaze pale-blue ground to the same four different white relief-moulded sprays as in pattern 2229 (Plate 87). The central fruit and the rim flowers are bat-prints overpainted with enamels. Added gold decoration.

Pattern 2359 *(Plate 371)*

Gold rim. Underglaze mazarine-blue, with orange for the two 'deer' and part of the houses. The rest of the decoration is gold.

Pattern 2679

Underglaze dark-blue ground to the same four different white relief-moulded sprays as in pattern 2229 (Plate 87). Added gold and enamelled bat-prints of flowers on the flanges. Peach-coloured enamel swags edged with gold surround the main decoration of painted 'Dr Syntax' scenes.

366.   Pattern 1897. STAND for wicker-moulded London-shape teapot. Enamelled pattern number.
Length 19.1 cm (7.5 in), 1825–30.

367.   Pattern 1934. COVERED PRESERVE-DISH. Enamelled pattern number.
Height 11.4 cm (4.5 in), 1820–30. *Godden Collection. See page 103.*

368. Pattern 1944. Wicker-moulded
      London-shape TEAPOT. Enamelled
      pattern number.
      Height 19.1 cm (7.5 in), 1825–30.

370. Pattern 2240. DESSERT-PLATE.
      Diameter 21.6 cm (8.5 in), 1825–30.
      Godden Collection.

369. Pattern 2155. DESSERT-PLATE. Enamelled
      pattern number.
      Diameter 21.6 cm (8.5 in), 1825–30.
      Godden Collection.

371. Pattern 2359. London-shape JUG.
      Enamelled pattern number.
      Height 8.6 cm (3.4 in), 1820–30.
      See page 138.

APPENDIX I

Documents connected with Richard Champion

1. Letter from Josiah Wedgwood to Mr Bentley dated 24 January 1776; in the Wedgwood Papers deposited in Keele University Library.

To Mr Bentley   *Etruria 24 Jany 1776*

My Dear Friend

. . . I mentioned to you once, that notwithstanding *Fritt Porcelain* had been so much decried, I thought the best method of making it would be from a Fritt, and I am more fully convinced of it by almost every experiment I make upon the subject.

There has been very imperfect Porcelains made with a Fritt of Sand, Salts, and Glass, from which the French Authors have drawn a hasty, and I think, false conclusion – That all Porcelains composed of Fritt and Clay must be imperfect, and False Porcelains, because, say they, the mixture would be converted into Glass by pushing the fire a little farther than the point they stop at to produce the ware they call Porcelain.

I believe this to be true of nearly all our present compositions in England and France, except the Bristol, and I believe salts should not enter into a Fritt, as they accelerate a too rapid vitrification, and though I would prohibit the use of Salts in a Body, I would nevertheless compose a Fritt, and that of the simplest materials, such as I could be certain of obtaining at any time of the same qualities, and this Fritt when burnt should have the qualities of *Felt Spar*, or the white parts of the *best Moor Stone*.

If I can compose such a Fritt as the above from *simple materials* I shall prefer it much to any compound of Natures Mixing; for she never weighs her materials, and I have never yet seen any of her Moor Stone or other compounds, which I could depend on having twice alike, even from the same Quarries.

By *Simple Materials*, I do not mean anything absolutely so, as you will readily imagine. But there are certain substances which approach near enough to that character for my purpose. Such as Bone-ashes, Black Flints, Lime, Alabastre, Chalk, and some others. I dare not rank 19 or Spath Fusible in this Class, but 74 may perhaps be admitted. Quartz I am in doubt about, as there are certainly various kinds of it. But I am trying all the different specimens I can procure, and hope you will furnish me with one or two soon.

When I have managed my Fritt, it is to make true Porcelain with a due proportion of Clay, and this Porcelain must have the quality of proceeding very slowly from one degree of vitrification to another, which is all that the best can boast of *Infusibility*.

The *infusibility* of the Oriental and Dresden Porcelain depends, perhaps, more upon the proportions in which the materials are compounded, than upon the Materials themselves, at least I am pretty certain of this, that *different proportions* of the *same Materials* will make *fusible* and *infusible* Porcelain.

I have given you my idea of the best plan for making *perfect Porcelain* with uniform success, and it is the plan I intend to proceed upon as time will permit, but I may probably make a *white ware* for Painting before the other plan is perfected into Manufacture.

As Moor Stone varies so much, being a compound, mixed at random perhaps by the waves and Tides of the Ocean, I despair of making it a Principal ingredient in a Porcelain Manufactory, and unless the Bristol People alter their principle I do not think it possible for them to succeed.

I will send you some Pitchers of 74 Porcelain and beg you will let Mr Rhodes try his skill in glazing them. . . .

. . . believe me ever yours most affectionately

Jos. Wedgwood

2. An Address by Richard Champion to the Pottery, April 1781; in the Wedgwood/Mosley 1853 Papers deposited in Keele University Library.

A consideration of the disadvantages which the Propriator of the Bristol China Manufactory labours under, from the situation in which his Works are placed, has induced him to compare the Prices he pays for Labour and Materials, with those of other established Potteries. On the Comparison he finds, that their Workmen are not only better, but their Wages little more than *one half*, the price of the essential Article of Coal *a fourth part alone*, and raw Materials in general, *in the same proportion*. Such a very great difference has determined him to change his Situation, being fully convinced that, manufacturing now to advantage in as *simple a manner as Earthen Ware and with as little Risque*, the savings alone will be a capital Sum. He has two Situations in view. The one is a neighbouring County, where Manufactures of Earthen Ware, similar to this Pottery, are carried on, where Coal is still cheaper, Workmen and raw Materials good and in plenty, *with* the advantage of being nearer the Sea for Export; and attended with this additional and weighty Circumstance, that all Countries, where Manufactures have been newly and successfully established, are continually desirous of Increase, *and peculiarly favourable to rising Works*. The other is the old and experienc'd Potteries in Staffordshire, where Coal and raw Materials are also cheap, where there are Numbers of Workmen, of excellence in every Branch. The observations which he has made since he has been in Staffordshire, seem to point it out to him as a very eligible Situation for his Manufactory to be removed to. His Sentiments have been considerably strengthened by the opinions of many very respectable Potters, who are not only desirous of encouraging it, but have express'd their wishes *that it may be extended on the most enlarged Scale; that the whole Pottery, and of course the Neighbourhood, may reap the greater Benefit from it*. To Public Utility he shall very chearfully give up every contracted Plan of his own; for, from his first application to the Discovery, the Improvement, and the Perfection of the Manufacture, he has spared neither Time, Pains, or Expense, his first Object having been to make it a great National Concern. If he should not be so fortunate, during the term which has been granted him, as to be repaid the very great but necessary Expences which he has been at in bringing so important a Manufacture to Perfection, his Country will be the Gainer; *for this Ware must be as common in England as it is in China itself*. Nor has he a doubt, should he come to an agreement with the Potters, but that *Staffordshire China will not only be the common Consumption of the Kingdom, but of every part of Europe and America to which the Cream Coloured Ware is exported, made with as little Trouble and Expence, and sufficiently cheap to prevent all future Importations from the East Indies*. He shall on his part very readily concur with the Pottery at large, in forming an extensive work in Shares by Subscription, open to the Country, or in any other manner that may forward an undertaking so productive of advantages, not only in a National View, but to the Parties who may be concern'd in it. He therefore submits to them the following Considerations.

FIRST. That this Porcelain or China Ware is manufactured *from a Native Clay*, of a hard and firm Texture, the Glaze smooth, and of a beautiful White. The enamelled Colours in great Perfection, the blue and white very good. It will boil Water, and is not injured by the most frequent Use. It resembles more nearly the Dresden, being superior to East India China Ware. The fine Fabric of Séve in France, the Chelsea, Derby, Worcester, Salopian, Leostoffe, and all other Wares in England, called *English China, are frit Bodies, which the Scratch of a Knife, hot Water, or even the Change of Weather will affect*, and may be thus distinguished from this Manufacture – they will melt into a *Glass or vitreous Substance*, and lose their form and original appearance in a degree of heat, which this China Ware, agreeing in all properties with the East India and Dresden, will not only bear, but which is necessary to manufacture it.

SECONDLY. That the Clay used in manufacturing this China Ware is of the most tenacious Nature, *and may be worked on the Wheel and Lathe, or pressed in Moulds, with the same ease as the common Clay* from which the Earthen Ware of this Country is made.

THIRDLY. That although the Fire, which is necessary to bring so fine a body to Perfection, is much greater than what is requisite for the Manufacture of Cream Coloured Ware, *yet it is not carried to the Height of the White Stone Kilns*. Besides there is a great Probability of lessening it in time, *to having been reduced within a very short Period nearly one half*. Another Circumstance strengthens this Opinion – there is a Species of Nankin China Ware, which is of a similar Nature to this, yet does not to appearance receive a greater degree of Heat than the Cream Coloured Ware, the Body (which is of a real China Ware, and which a greater degree of Fire will make transparent) *having a Suction, yet it is perfect, and of a fine Quality*.

FOURTHLY. That this China Ware is manufactured with as much certainty, and the Kilns are as productive, as the Cream Coloured Kilns, *an equal Quantity of good Ware being produced from them*.

FIFTHLY. That all the Disadvantages which have occurred in the Discovery and Progress of this Work, *now of above Thirty Years Continuance, and at the Expence of near Thirty Thousand Pounds*, have been for some time wholly at an end, and a great and extensive Sale has been made, both *in elegant Table and Desert Services; and all sorts of useful and ornamental Ware, with an* increasing Reputation. The Manufacture therefore is not to be considered as an Experimental one, but as an *Established Work*, removing from one Country to another, merely for the Benefit of better and cheaper Workmen and Materials; and with this advantage to those who receive it, that they have no Share in the heavy Burthen which has attended its formation.

SIXTHLY.   That the Establishment of this Manufactory in the Potteries, *by introducing a different System of Manufacture, in the management of Fire, the Construction of Kilns, and the use of new Materials, will make such essential Improvement in all kinds of Earthen Ware, as will form an entire System of Pottery*; and will be the means of preventing the *considerable Expence* which every Potter is at in Experiments, amounting *annually* amongst the whole *to a very large Sum of Money*.

3.   Transcription by W. J. Pountney of four letters written by Richard Champion; now in the Bristol Record Office. (I believe that the originals are deposited in the Swedenborg Institute (Sw/A 143).)

(a) (From Richard Champion to James Fox. Original letter and signature.)

Dear Sir,
You have formerly given me reason to experience your friendship, and tho' what I have now to say is about your Relations cousin Cookworthy, and her sisters, I do it without apology, as they are our mutual friends, and I am well convinced your knowledge of the affair makes you the properest Person to consult.

    You know that I exchanged the old Terms of the China, for the same rent that was paid Mr Pitt for the materials, of which some was paid to the late Mr Cookworthy, and there is now more (though not a great deal) due, but the amount I cannot say as I am from home, having just left Staffordshire, and being now at Lord Rockingham's for a few days.

    I designed to have wrote you from thence where I was about a week, but was prevented by continual Imployment amongst the Potters (with whom I was in the Spring above two months negotiating a Plan for the introduction of my

Porcelain Manufactory), and therefore took the opportunity whilst I am here and more at leisure. I have made Proposals, which are under Consideration. But there are such general Complaints of the dearness of the raw Materials, that the affair has been much at a stand, and I have been obliged to write to Mr Pitt, who has given me reason to understand on his part, that he will make an abatement. When you consider that the Potters have now a Lease of good Materials, close to St Stephens, at only 12 gs p year and when Carthew will also sell them good nearly at the rate of common pipe-clay, you may easily suppose what Chance I shall have in carrying on a Manufactory, when it becomes general in Staffordshire, which is part of the Plan.

It is impossible to oblige the Potters to use my Materials. They will go where it is cheapest. I am induced therefore to consult you upon the occasion, to know the Sentiments of Your Cousins, whether it would not be most for our mutual advantage, to come to some specific agreement for the term of the Patent, which expires in 1796.

We should all undoubtedly make the most we can, but we ought not for our own sakes to uphold a false Glare of advantage, whilst we are losing the real fruits. The present plan has a Clause in it, giving Liberty to every Potter to make the Porcelain in his own works, on payment of a certain fine to the Company. No Power can oblige them to buy the Material, but a Moderate Price, when it is likely they might be induced to purchase them by good Management. This I have told Mr Pitt plainly, and I think it proper to request you to mention to your Cousins. You are sensible that one Consequence of the use of other Clay must be, the old Work will drop from its particular Disadvantages, in which case the Lease will fall into Mr Pitt's hands, and your Cousins' claim being grafted upon it, will sink in course. It therefore becomes a mutual benefit to sell the Clay as cheap as possible.

I will not detain you too long. I believe what I have said will give you the general Ideas. They know what has already been received. £120 from the year 1774 to 1778. Since that time it has been much less, or is there a Chance in the present Circumstances of making it otherwise than a trifling object, and the only way to create even a permanency of it, or afford a mutual advantage is to fix upon some specific Plan for the term of the Patent, which I beg you to procure me their Sentiments upon, and send me an answer directed to me in Bristol, where I shall be about the 15th. I shall thank you to make my best respects to Mrs Fox and all your family, and that you would remember me to your Cousin Lydia, and her sisters who are with her.

I wish you to be assured that I am with great truth dear sir,
    Your obliged and Sincere friend
      Rich: Champion
Wentworth House
Yorkshire.
6 Aug^{st.} 1781.

(b) George Harrison will be obliged to his cousin James Fox to inform Richard Champion that the Executors of Wm. Cookworthy are disposed to promote his views in introducing the China Manufactory among the People of Staffordshire and should be glad [if] R. C. would write him fully respecting the terms upon which he would propose to put the Business into their Hands as far as regards the Exors. Claim upon the Manufactory.
      No. 5. Fish St Hill 22nd 8mo.81.
(The above is copied from a draft for a letter – full of corrections.)

(c) (Autograph letter from Richard Champion to 'Mr George Harrison No. 5/Fish Street Hill.' Sealed in red wax with a coat of arms.)

                  Henbury near Bristol
                  3 Sept. 1780? [1781]
Sir,
Our mutual friend Mr Fox has given me your letter to him of the 22nd August; in consequence of which I shall give you my Sentiments upon the Occasion, principally in the manner I did to him. When I first went into Staffordshire in the Spring my views were considerably more enlarged than they are at present. I intended to have established a large work, and if Mr Wedgwood would have supported it, I might have done it. But this opposition prevented me and I have now entered into an agreement with ten Potters only, who if they like the Manufactory on its Establishment in the County are to give me a certain sum for liberty to use it in their own works, but I have also liberty to sell to any other I please on the original Plan for a Company, there was a clause designed to be inserted, that every Potter who belonged to it, should have on payment of a certain fine, liberty to make China in his Works.

In this situation I naturally looked to some Advantages from the sale of Materials but the high price of them, compared with those of Trethewys (Twelve guineas a year) and Carthews equally cheap, made me have very little hopes of advantage.

The Potters who knew the prices and your claim made this a capital objection to a Company, I therefore laid the case fairly before Mr Pitt, who was equally concerned with me, with respect to the use of his Materials. He wrote me that he would make any reasonable Abatement.

The case stands thus with all of us, I have a lease from Mr Pitt for 99 years, you have the same claim from me as he receives for the Materials, but I carry on the smallest work, the advantages you will either receive will be trifling. Again, if I carry on no work, the Lease falls into Mr Pitt's hands, he may make what Bargain he pleases with fresh Leasees, or sell his Materials, and your Claim sinks in course, as it only exists with my Lease, which is Determinable on my carrying on the work or not.

Mr Pitt is certainly in the worst Situation if I do, because the tax which I consented to lay on his Materials by my Agreement with Mr Cookworthy, makes the Materials cost so much (and being a perpetuity without a possibility of its ceasing) that in its present state it must naturally throw the sale of Materials into other hands to his great Injury.

The Remidy comes next, I wish to reap Advantage naturally from the sale of Materials. I wish equally for you. Mr Pitt must do the same. But strong as all our Wishes are, I see no Method than your consenting to restrain your claim to a certain period on such a certain price per annum as we can agree on. But to settle this arises fresh Difficulties. Hitherto what has arisen to you has been very trifling. In future if I could render the Materials tolerably cheap, it may increase. But if this is not to be done, it must be a total loss to all you and me, as Mr Pitt may by my not being [able] to carry on the Work, enter into fresh Agreements.

At present he seems willing to agree to reasonable Terms. You will please always to carry this in your View, that the Potters will buy when[1] they please, and that there is no other way of engaging them than by selling cheap.

I have said sufficient on this occasion to make you Master of the subject, when you have considered it, you will be so good as to write me your Sentiments.

I beg to be remembered particularly to Mrs Harrison and your sister Lydia who is with you and that you will believe me to be your sincere friend and servant

Richard Champion

(Note that although the transcript gives the date as 1780 the date must really have been 1781 for the letters to be in sequence.)

---

[1] Presumably this should be 'where'.

(d) (Draft of copy of a letter from George Harrison to Richard Champion in reply to last. This letter is not completed.)

To Richd Champion, Bristol. Sep. 19th. 1781.

Respected Frd,

I am obliged to thee for the information contained in thy Favour of the 3rd. Inst, relative to the China Business and in case any determinate Plan of prosecuting it should be fix't on shall be very willing to promote thy views of Advantage, as far as I can consistent with the just Claim of those concerned as W.C.'s Representatives, to whose consideration I shall very cheerfully submit any terms thou may propose either upon the Plan of retaining their claim to a certain Period or to a certain Price per annum which ever may be most compatable with thy views, & I doubt not their compliance with reasonable Terms.

I own I am not yet perfectly inform'd on what Ground their claim rests, but as it is for the *Merit of Invention* I shou'd presume that whilst any Advantage arises to thee from the *Manufacture*, whether by way of a Fine from the Potters, or from the sale of Materials, their claim will be valid in some proportion but on this subject I may probably be further inform'd ere anything more passes between us.

4.   Policy 546 in the Salop Fire Office Records: Book 1, page 261:

Richard Champion Esq of Newcastle in the County of Stafford Porcelain Manufacturer desires to Insure

		£
1.	On Household Goods in his now Dwelling House only situate in Merrill Street, Brick and tiled not exceeding Two Hundred Pounds	200
2.	Wearing Apparel therein only not exceeding One Hundred Pounds	100
3.	Printed Books therein only not exceeding One Hundred Pounds	100
4.	China therein only not exceeding One Hundred Pounds	100
5.	Utensils and Stock in trade consisting of Cobbalt and Blue Colour prepared therein only not exceeding Four Hundred Pounds	400
6.	Laboratory separate Brick and Tiled not exceeding One Hundred Pounds	100
		£1,000

	£		£	s	d
Art 1, 2, 3, 5	800 at 2/–		0	16	0
Art 6	100 " "		0	3	0
Art 4	100 " "		0	5	0
N.P.	Annual Premium		£1	4	0
	Policy Fee		£0	14	0
			£1	18	0

Documents in the William Salt Library, Stafford

The most relevant documents in the William Salt Library (Folio number D1798/536) which were consulted in the writing of Chapter 4:

–/1/1 14 July 1773. The Copyhold surrender of Shelton Hall and surrounds by Alice Dalton of London to Humphrey Palmer of Hanley, Potter. At this time there were nine named parcels of land. (In the 1803 agreement there was a reduction to seven named parcels of land although the total area remained the same.)

–/1/2 4 September 1777. Humphrey Palmer, the Copyholder, settles the property on his intended wife Hannah Ashwin. Thomas Palmer is a tenant at £30 per annum rent.

–/1/3 30 September 1789. Humphrey Palmer and his widow Hannah are dead and their daughter Mary takes copyhold possession of the property.

–/1/4 2 November 1802. Miss Mary Palmer surrenders the property on lease to Messrs Hollins and Co., China Manufacturers and copartners '. . . wherein they carry on their China Manufactory'.

–/1/5 1 March 1803. 'Articles of agreement made this first day of March 1803 between Mary Palmer of Birmingham in the County of Warwick, spinster, of the one hand, and John Hollins of Newcastle-under-Lyme, in the County of Stafford, Gentleman, Samuel Hollins of Shelton in the said County, Potter, Peter Warburton of Wolstanton in the said County, potter, William Clowes of Porthill in the said County, Gentleman, Joshua Heath and Charles Bagnall of Shelton aforesaid, Gentlemen, and John Daniel of Shelton aforesaid, Potter, Copartners together under the firm of Hollins, Warburton, Daniel and Company of the other part as follows: . . .' Mary Palmer promises to the partners to 'surrender into the hands of the Lord of the said Manor . . . All that Building and Tenement called the New Hall formerly used and occupied as a Dwelling House but now converted and used as a China Warehouse together with the Hovels Workshops Manufactory and Buildings belonging thereto. And also all those seven several Closes pieces or parcels of land lying together and adjoining to the said Buildings and premises . . . twenty-nine acres or thereabouts . . . and are now in the occupation of the said Hollins Warburton Daniel and Company together with full and free liberty power and authority to and for the said Hollins Warburton Daniel and Company to get and use Marl from the said premises for the use of the said China Manufactory at all times. . . . To hold the said Manufactory Hovels Buildings . . . during the Term of fourteen years pay or cause to be paid unto the said Mary Palmer . . . the yearly rent or sum of two hundred and ten pounds clear of all deductions whatsoever . . . and also further yearly rent or sum of eight pounds per cent for all money to be hereafter laid out and expended by the said Mary Palmer . . . in erecting new buildings for the Use of the Manufactory. . . . And also that they . . . at their own costs . . . maintain amend and keep in good and substantial order and repair . . . the said Manufactory Hovels Warehouses Workshops . . . Damage by or in consequence of the working of the Coal Mines under the said premises only excepted. . . . And also that the said Mary Palmer . . . will pay unto the said John Hollins . . . sums of money (not exceeding in the whole the sum of three hundred pounds) which they shall require for the purpose of erecting new buildings to the said Manufactory . . . Provided lastly . . . that if the said Mary Palmer . . . shall at any time during the first seven years of the said term of fourteen years actually dispose of the said premises and shall signify the same to the said John Hollins . . . by notice in writing . . . for the space of twenty four Calendar months at least before the end of the said seventh year In such case the said Term of fourteen years . . . shall cease . . . Or if the said John Hollins . . . shall be desirous to determine and make void the said term of fourteen years at the end of the seventh year of the said term and shall signify such their intention to the said Mary Palmer . . . by notice in writing . . . for the space of twenty four Calendar months at least before the end of the said seventh year In such case the said Term of fourteen years . . . shall cease. . . .'

–/1/6 and –/1/7 15 February 1806. The will of Mary Palmer (dated 21 December 1805) is presented to Court. The New Hall China Manufactory is mentioned as the tenants.

−/1/13 27 April 1810. Deed of Covenant and release of the Copyhold Estate from Ester and Elizabeth Palmer and James Neale to Hollins, Warburton Daniel and Co. for £6,800. (James Neale was involved because he had given one of the sisters a £2,800 mortgage on the property.)

−/1/14 14 August 1814. The property and Pottery (known as the New Hall Company) is surrendered to John Daniel.

−/1/16 17 February 1821. Following the death of John Daniel, Alice Daniel (his sister) surrenders the New Hall Manufactory and its lands to William Clowes.

−/1/17 and −/1/18 26 August 1823 and 13 October 1824. Presentment of the death of William Clowes, Porthill and the surrender and admission of the property from the co-heiresses and their husbands to Hugh Henshall Williamson.

−/5/12 7 January 1843. Surrender and admittance of the buildings and the remainder of the estate by Hugh Henshall Williamson (on behalf of the New Hall Company) to William Loftus Lowndes of London for the sum of £3,050.

−/5/13 7 January 1843. A fourteen year lease by William Loftus Lowndes to William and Thomas Hackwood for £225 per annum. William and Thomas Hackwood leased 'All that capital Earthenware Manufactory called the New Hall Manufactory consisting of five Hovels three Sliphouses and two hardening hovels together with all and singular the warehouses Workshops Machine House and other buildings and erections thereto belonging and together also with the Marl Bank Clay yards and other yards lands and grounds hereditaments and premises thereto also belonging situate at Shelton within the said Manor of Newcastle-under-Lyme in the County of Stafford and late in the tenure or occupation of William Ratcliffe. Together with all and singular the fixtures and articles comprised in the schedule hereunder written. . . .'

The schedule lists thirty-one places which contain fixtures and articles. 'No 1 Large Warehouse. No 2 Best Warehouse. No 3 Warehouse. No 4 Biscuit Warehouse. No 5 Dipping House. No 6 Lead House. No 8 Painting Shop. No 9 Printing Shop. No 10 Printers Hot House. No 11 Throwing House and Soaking room. No 12 New hot house. No 13 Turninghouse. No 17 and 18 White sliphouse. No 19 Squeezinghouse over the Biscuit Saggar house. No 20. No 21 The room over the last. No 22 Flagged Chamber over Saggar-hot-house. No 23 Saggar makers hot house. No 24 Saggar makers place. No 25 Dish makers place. No 26 Room over Clay cellar and the Greenhouse. No 27 Saucer makers place & rooms for squeezers. Dish Makers place. No 28 Clay Cellar near New Green House. No 29 The Clay Cellars under the Printing Stove and Hot house. No 30. No 31.'

Insurance Policies taken out by New Hall

Insurance Policies taken out by New Hall and preserved in the Salop Fire Office Records in the possession of the Sun Alliance Insurance Group, Shrewsbury.

22 March 1792

No. 1562

		£
Messrs Hollins Warburton and Co. of Hanley in the County of Stafford, Potters desire to Insure		
1.	On a Stock of China in their Pott-Works in one connected Range near New Hall in Hanley aforesaid not exceeding One Thousand Pounds	1,000
2.	Biscuit Ware therein only not exceeding Two Hundred Pounds	200
3.	Stock of China in Pott-Works in one connected Range at Booden Brook in Hanley aforesaid not exceeding Five Hundred Pounds	500
4.	Working Utensils in their Pottery at New Hall aforesaid only not exceeding One Hundred Pounds N.B. All Brick and Tiled	100
		£1,800

	£	£ s d
Art. 1, 2, 3	1,700 at 5/–	4 5 0
Art. 4	100 at 3/–	0 3 0
		─────────
	Annual Premium	4 8 0
	Policy Fea	0 14 0
		─────────
		£5 2 0
		─────────

		£
1.	April 13th 1793 The Stock of china Ware Art 1 above mentioned being removed to the New Building in Hanley aforesaid Brick and Tiled continue to be Insured there only, and	1,000
3.	The Stock of China Art 3 being removed from Booden Brook to the New Hall House continue Insured there only, and by desire of the parties reduced to Four Hundred Pounds	400
2.	The Biscuit Ware therein not exceeding One Hundred Pounds	100
5.	Stock of plain China in the White Warehouse and painting shops only not exceeding Two Hundred Pounds	200
4.	Art 4 continue as before	100
		£1,800

September 11th 1793 Messrs Hollins Warburton & Co. desire to add to their insurance

6. On a Dwelling House Barn and two Stables connected Brick and Tiled not exceeding One Hundred Pounds   £100

   Total Sum Insured £1,900 – Annual Premium £4 11 0.

7 November 1810

No. 10,264

Messrs Hollins Warburton Daniel and Clowes of New Hall in Shelton and Cty of Stafford, China Manufacturers desire to insure

		£
1.	their manufactory in one connected range situate as above, not exceeding £900	£900
2.	their stock of china therein not exceeding £900	£900
3.	their utensils and fixtures therein not exceeding £200	£200

4. their dwelling house called New Hall House situate near the above
manufactory – not exceeding £300   £300
5. their stock of china therein, not exceeding £600   £600
6. their barn stable and small house situate near to the premises
aforesaid – not exceeding £100   £100
All the above described buildings are of brick and slate.

Amount insured   £3,000

Art. 1, 3, 4   £1400 at 2/–   =   £1   8   0
     6   100 at 3/–   3   0
     2 & 5   1500 at 5/–   3   15   0

Annual Premium   £5   6   0

Memorandum. Aug 15th 1812. Art. 4 being taken down, the insurance thereon is discontinued, and in view thereof, their warehouses, packing house & two counting houses under the same roof situate near Article 6 is to stand insured at the sum. Amount insured and annual premium as before.
Sept. 29th 1826 Annual premium reduced to £4 11 0d.

BIBLIOGRAPHY

BOOKS

W. A. Pitt, *Topographical History of Staffordshire*, London, 1817

Simeon Shaw, *History of the Staffordshire Potteries*, Hanley, 1829

J. Ward, *The Borough of Stoke-on-Trent*, London, 1843

John Prideaux, *William Cookworthy*, Plymouth, 1853

George Harrison, *Memoir of William Cookworthy*, London, 1854

H. Owen, *Two Centuries of Ceramic Art in Bristol*, London, 1873

Llewellynn Jewitt, *The Ceramic Art of Great Britain*, 2 vols., London 1878

J. C. Wedgwood, *Staffordshire Pottery and its History*, London, 1913

H. Eccles and B. Rackham, *Analysed Specimens of English Porcelain*, London (Victoria and Albert Museum), 1922.

F. Severne MacKenna, *Cookworthy's Plymouth and Bristol Porcelain*, Leigh-on-Sea, 1946

F. Severne MacKenna, *Champion's Bristol Porcelain*, Leigh-on-Sea, 1947

G. E. Stringer, *New Hall Porcelain*, London, 1949

R. G. Haggar, *The Masons of Lane Delph*, London, 1952

R. G. Haggar and W. Mankowitz, *The Concise Encyclopaedia of English Pottery and Porcelain*, London, 1957

R. J. Charleston (editor), *English Porcelain 1745–1850*, London, 1965

B. Hillier, *The Turners of Lane End*, London, 1965

R. M. Barton, *A History of the Cornish China Clay Industry*, Truro, 1966

D. Holgate, *New Hall and Its Imitators*, London, 1971

B. M. Watney, *English Blue and White Porcelain of the Eighteenth Century*, 2nd ed., London, 1973

A. D. Selleck, *Cookworthy 1705–80 and his Circle*, Plymouth, 1978

Geoffrey Godden (editor), *Staffordshire Porcelain*, St Albans, 1983

Another list of books is given at the end of Chapter 8.

ARTICLES

F. H. Rhead, 'New Hall china', *Connoisseur*, vol. XLVI, September–December 1916, pp. 221–4

W. H. Tapp, 'Fidelle Duvivier: ceramic artist', *Apollo*, vol. XXXII, December 1940, pp. 160–3, and ibid., vol. XXXIII, March 1941, pp. 57–9

T. A. Sprague, 'Hard-paste New Hall porcelain', *Apollo*, vol. XLIX, June 1949, pp. 165–7; ibid., vol. L, July 1949, pp. 16–18; ibid., LII, August 1950, pp. 51–4; ibid., vol. LII, October 1950, pp. 109–12; 'Black transfers on bone-paste porcelain', ibid., vol. LXIII, March 1956, pp. 85–6; 'New light on polychrome Caughley', ibid., vol. LXIX, January 1959, pp. 14–17; 'Hard-paste New Hall porcelain', *English Ceramic Circle Transactions (E.C.C. Trans.)*, vol. 3, part 3, 1954, pp. 123–8

R. G. Haggar, 'New Hall – the last phase', *Apollo*, vol. LIV, November 1951, pp. 133–7

R. J. Charleston, 'The end of Bristol. The beginning of New Hall: some fresh evidence', *Connoisseur*, April 1956, pp. 185–8

G. A. Godden, 'Caughley teawares painted by Fidelle Duvivier. The missing link', *Antique Dealer and Collector's Guide*, August 1978, pp. 67–70

Geoffrey Grey, 'New Hall, Hand-paste Porcelain', *English Ceramic Circle Transactions (E.C.C. Trans.)*, vol. 8, part 1, 1971, pp. 1–15.

D. F. Holgate, 'Polychrome and hard-paste Caughley porcelain', *English Ceramic Circle Transactions (E.C.C. Trans.)*, vol. 6, part 3, 1967, pp. 268–83; 'Fidelle Duvivier paints New Hall', ibid., vol. 11, part 1, 1981, pp. 12–20

Kit Holgate, 'New Hall Porcelain', *Antique Dealer and Collector's Guide*, October 1965, pp. 42–8; 'New Hall Niceties', *Antique Collecting*, October 1983, pp. 8–11

Kit Holgate and G. A. Godden, 'The Total Look of New Hall', *Antique Dealer and Collector's Guide*, April 1971, pp. 62–74

F. Severne MacKenna, 'William Cookworthy and the Plymouth factory', *English Ceramic Circle Transactions (E.C.C. Trans.)*, vol. 11, part 2, 1982, p. 84–98

INDEX